Pathways to Religious Life

Edited by Thomas P. Gaunt, SJ

OXFORD
UNIVERSITY PRESS

OXFORD
UNIVERSITY PRESS

Oxford University Press is a department of the University of Oxford. It furthers
the University's objective of excellence in research, scholarship, and education
by publishing worldwide. Oxford is a registered trade mark of Oxford University
Press in the UK and certain other countries.

Published in the United States of America by Oxford University Press
198 Madison Avenue, New York, NY 10016, United States of America.

Library of Congress Cataloging-in-Publication Data
Names: Gaunt, Thomas P., editor.
Title: Pathways to religious life / edited by Thomas Gaunt.
Description: New York, NY : Oxford University Press, 2018. |
Includes bibliographical references and index.
Identifiers: LCCN 2017057393 (print) | LCCN 2018020806 (ebook) |
ISBN 9780190878160 (updf) | ISBN 9780190878177 (epub) |
ISBN 9780190878184 (online resource) | ISBN 9780190878153 (hardcover : alk. paper)
Subjects: LCSH: Monasticism and religious orders—United States. |
Monastic and religious life. | Vocation—Catholic Church.
Classification: LCC BX2505 (ebook) | LCC BX2505 .P38 2018 (print) |
DDC 255—dc23
LC record available at https://lccn.loc.gov/2017057393

9 8 7 6 5 4 3 2 1

Printed by Sheridan Books, Inc., United States of America

Contents

Figures

Tables

Contributors

⌒

Thu T. Do is a Sister of the Lovers of the Holy Cross-Hanoi from Vietnam. She recently finished her doctoral study in Higher Education Administration at Saint Louis University. Her research interests include Catholic higher education, college student formation, and international religious sisters in the United States.

Thomas P. Gaunt is a Jesuit priest and Executive Director of CARA. He has served in Jesuit governance as the Socius/Executive Secretary of the Jesuit Conference-USA and was the Formation and Studies Director of the Maryland and New York Jesuit Provinces. After ordination, he spent ten years as a pastor and as Director of Planning and Research in the Diocese of Charlotte.

Mary L. Gautier is a sociologist and Senior Research Associate at CARA. She specializes in Catholic demographic trends in the United States. She edits The CARA Report and other CARA publications. She is co-author of nine books on U.S. Catholicism, most recently *Catholic Parishes of the 21st Century*.

Jonathon Holland is a doctoral student at the University of Louisville. He was a Research Associate at CARA prior to beginning his doctoral studies. His current research interests include quantitative research methods and organizations.

Mary Johnson is a Sister of Notre Dame de Namur and Professor of Sociology and Religious Studies at Trinity Washington University in Washington, DC. Previously she was on the faculty of Emmanuel College in Boston. She is co-author of *Young Adult Catholics: Religion in a Culture of Choice* and *New Generations of Catholic Sisters: The Challenge of Diversity*, as well as numerous articles on Catholicism.

Patricia Wittberg is a Sister of Charity of Cincinnati Ohio. She holds a PhD in sociology from the University of Chicago and is currently a Research Associate with the Center for Applied Research in the Apostolate. She is the author of numerous books and articles on Catholicism and Catholic religious life, most recently *Catholic Cultures*.

1

An Overview of the History of Religious Life in the United States

Patricia Wittberg and Thomas P. Gaunt

THE 2,000-YEAR-LONG HISTORY of religious life in the Catholic Church has been filled with changes: periods of membership growth and decline, shifts in the types of ministries that religious orders engaged in, and differences in the ethnic and socioeconomic backgrounds of the men and women who joined them. Religious life in the United States has experienced all of these changes during the past two centuries and is continuing to do so today. The Center for Applied Research in the Apostolate (CARA) at Georgetown University has charted some of the changing features of religious life in the United States and has released several reports on its findings. Recently, CARA received a grant from the Conrad N. Hilton Foundation to compile these reports into the present book, and to reflect on the implications of its research findings for religious life today.

This chapter will briefly describe the history of religious life in the United States, focusing on the many changes it has experienced, in order to place the present situation of U.S. religious orders in a broader context. Subsequent chapters will discuss the changes in membership, types of ministry, and the sources of vocations that men's and women's religious institutes are experiencing today in the United States. The final chapter will outline some of the implications of these changes for religious institutes as they face the future.

CHANGES IN RELIGIOUS LIFE BEFORE 1950
Changing Demographics

The first male religious[1] to arrive in North America were French Jesuits and Spanish Franciscans, who initially ministered in Canada and Mexico, respectively, during the sixteenth and seventeenth centuries. Soon after their arrival, both orders spread into what is now the United States, with the English Jesuits arriving in the colony of Maryland in 1634. Women religious, too, appeared in Canada and Mexico during this time, and by 1727 the first convent of sisters was founded in a city—New Orleans—that would later become part of the United States. The Ursuline sisters in this first convent opened a school as soon as they arrived and began engaging in home nursing as well. In 1734 they also opened the first Catholic hospital in the soon-to-be United States. Later in the 1700s, a group of cloistered Carmelite nuns came to Maryland at the invitation of Bishop John Carroll, and a group of Visitation sisters opened a school for girls. Throughout the eighteenth century, however, the number of male and female religious in the United States was extremely small.

This changed during the nineteenth century. In 1820, there were only about 270 women religious in the entire country, and only 150 priests (secular diocesan priests and religious order priests combined). By 1850, however, the number of sisters had increased fivefold to 1,344 women religious in nineteen separate religious congregations, while priests numbered about 1,800. By 1900, there were 40,340 sisters in forty-five different religious congregations (Wittberg 1994:39).[2] The number of men in religious orders and the diocesan priesthood was fewer than the number of sisters, but it too had greatly increased from about 1,800 in 1850 to nearly 12,000 in 1900 (Dolan 1985:277).

The socioeconomic background of those who entered religious orders changed over this time period as well. Prior to 1820, sisters had come primarily from middle- to upper-class Catholic families who had lived in the United States for generations, while many of the priests were already-ordained British, Irish, and French clergy who were fleeing persecution in their homelands (Misner 1988:107). With the beginning of the great waves of immigration in the mid- to late-nineteenth century, however, more and more sisters and priests came from the immigrant working class. By the late nineteenth century, over 90 percent of the sisters in

---

[1] This term, and the term "women religious" below, refer to any Catholic man or woman who has professed some sort of canonically-recognized vow or promise to observe a certain way of life. The most commonly-recognized vows (but not the only ones) are poverty, chastity, and obedience.

[2] In New York City alone, the eighty-two sisters who ministered there in 1848 had grown to 2,846 by 1898—three times the number of priests and brothers there.

places like Boston or New York were either immigrants themselves or the children of immigrants (Oates 1985:175; Wittberg 1994:69; Fitzgerald 2006:199). Few men and women religious came from middle- or upper-class backgrounds, although they did tend to be from a slightly better-off segment of the working class. Most had fathers who were craftsmen or farmers rather than unskilled laborers.

Different religious orders varied in the socioeconomic characteristics of their members. Some, like the Jesuits or the Religious of the Sacred Heart, taught wealthier students in their academies and "colleges,"[3] and therefore tended to attract wealthier entrants than orders that ministered primarily to the poor (Thompson 1989:152–153). This led to a sort of class distinction in the nineteenth and early twentieth centuries, in which some orders were considered more or less prestigious than others. The orders also varied in the ethnicity of their members: Those who ministered to Irish, German, or Polish immigrants drew their members largely from those they served (Fitzgerald 2006:21).

Religious who ministered in the United States often came here as adults, having already entered their communities before leaving Europe. Many U.S. bishops and priests were instrumental in bringing groups of women religious here and supporting them once they arrived. Since scores of new parishes were being established for the immigrants to America's burgeoning cities, priests and religious from their home countries, who spoke their language and were familiar with their culture, were needed to staff them. A bishop who did not provide for his flock would have been considered derelict in his duty. Likewise, a parish priest's status in his diocese, as well as his relationship with his largely immigrant parishioners who demanded education in the language and culture of their homeland, depended on his being a "brick and mortar" pastor. Sisters were needed to staff—and sometimes even to build—the institutions that the priests and bishops wanted to establish (Wittberg 1994:87). Nineteenth-century bishops accordingly visited motherhouses and seminaries in Europe to recruit sisters and diocesan seminarians for ministry in the United States. Both bishops and priests might also work with local laywomen to begin new congregations of religious in their diocese or parish.

Religious order priests, on the other hand, had a much cooler welcome than the sisters had. Bishops tended to be suspicious of male orders, since their members were subject to an international superior and not to the local Ordinary of the diocese. The bishops of Los Angeles and St. Paul, Minnesota, for example, engaged in ongoing feuds with the Franciscans and Jesuits: As late as the 1890s, "it was said

---

[3] In the nineteenth century, "colleges" for men resembled more the junior and senior high schools of today: They included six years, not four, and accepted boys as young as ten or twelve.

that a Jesuit dared not even change trains in St. Paul," so great was the archbishop's antipathy toward them (O'Connell 1989:112; Wittberg 1994:79).

Types of Ministry

In the largely Catholic countries of Europe, the ministries of men and women religious were supported by the state. Many long-established orders also had revenue from properties they had owned for centuries. Nineteenth-century men and women religious in the United States, on the other hand, had to support themselves financially. As a result of this economic necessity, many sisters established academies for wealthy Catholic and (more usually) Protestant girls, where they taught upper-class subjects such as French, music, needlework, and drawing. There was a great demand for such "finishing schools" by Protestant parents of the aspiring middle class. In 1810, the sisters ran ten such academies; by 1850, there were over a hundred (Wittberg 2006:26). The tuition from these establishments then supported free schools for the poor, which the sisters considered to be their most important ministry.

The "colleges" for boys and young men had a different origin and purpose. These educational institutions were primarily founded by the bishops as a way of recruiting and training desperately needed future priests. By 1830, fourteen such men's colleges had been founded and male orders recruited to staff them (Dolan 1985:249). The colleges followed the six-year European pattern and admitted students as young as eight years old as well as young men in their late teens. All were taught a basic classical curriculum, "ranging from elementary courses like spelling, penmanship, and basic English grammar to college-level work in Latin, Greek, and Philosophy" (Dolan 1985:250). These studies were considered less practical by Catholic and Protestant parents, who preferred to apprentice their sons as craftsmen or as clerks in business. By 1850, there were fewer than half as many men's colleges (forty-two) as there were women's academies. Most were small (100 to 150 students), financially precarious, and often short-lived (Glazier and Shelley 1997:250–251; Hutchison 2001:3).

In the early decades of the nineteenth century, there were few public elementary schools, and children were not obliged to attend even those that did exist. By mid-century, however, this had changed: More states were requiring at least a grade-school education for all children and were setting up public elementary schools to provide it. Catholic bishops were suspicious of the kind of education provided by the public schools, believing—correctly—they were strongly Protestant, or even blatantly anti-Catholic. Beginning with their First Plenary Council in 1852, the bishops began to encourage the establishment of a Catholic elementary school in every parish; this was made a mandate in the Third Plenary Council in 1884. The sisters then began to teach in these parish grade schools and ceased the operation of their separate free schools for the poor.

Throughout most of the nineteenth century, people who became ill or injured were cared for in their own homes, either by family members or by hired nurses. Hospitals were repositories for the indigent and unattached who had neither relatives to care for them nor money to pay anyone else to do so. Catholic women religious were often the only persons willing to care for such unfortunates. The sisters considered nursing to be a holy and meritorious work, caring for Christ Himself in the person of the sick poor. It was also an opportunity to bring dying patients to conversion and/or repentance, and to care for any children left behind after a parent's death. Since the hospitals and orphanages of the time served primarily the very poor, they were never self-supporting, and the sisters collected funds for them from local governments and private donors. By 1861, seventeen different congregations of women religious staffed thirty hospitals, both public municipal ones and those they owned themselves (Wittberg 2006:31). The reputation that the sisters earned for skilled nursing in these hospitals led to their recruitment as nurses during the Civil War: Of the 3,200 women who nursed the Northern and Southern soldiers, 640 were sisters. The unselfish service of women religious in the Civil War was a key factor in breaking down the intense anti-Catholicism that had previously existed in the United States.

By 1900, American sisters owned or staffed a wide range of educational, health care, and social service institutions: 3,811 parochial schools, 633 girls' academies, 645 orphanages, and over 500 hospitals (Wittberg 1994:34). The male orders were also heavily involved in colleges, in evangelization work, and in preaching yearly revivalistic "missions" in parishes around the country. Between 1850 and 1900, 152 new Catholic colleges were established in the United States by the men's religious orders (Hutchison 2001:3).

By and large, the Catholic schools and hospitals of nineteenth-century America were entirely staffed and administered by the religious orders. Sisters, brothers, and religious priests comprised the entire faculty and administration of their schools, academies, and colleges. The sisters who worked in hospitals not only did all the nursing; they also "managed the garden, the cow, the laundry and the cooking, as well as . . . collecting tours to raise money." The sisters "grew the food, harvested it, preserved and/or prepared it. They sewed linens for beds and [washed them] weekly" (Moylan 1993:40–41). Young men and women religious were assigned to positions in these institutions directly upon leaving the novitiate, and were mentored in the skills they would need by older and more experienced members. Sisters and religious priests or brothers who showed talent in

their early posts would be subsequently mentored and promoted to higher administrative positions.

Throughout the nineteenth and into the twentieth century, the United States
was considered a mission country. Religious order priests and brothers, accordingly, performed a wide range of roles beyond the traditional ministries they had
performed in Europe. The sisters, moreover, were not considered "real" religious,
since they took only simple rather than solemn vows. Relatively free from cloister
restrictions, and serving in burgeoning cities or in rapidly expanding frontier
areas, they committed themselves to meet "whatever need presents itself," as one
early sister in the New Mexico territory put it (Segale 1948:33). True to this entrepreneurial spirit, they did not merely teach in schools or nurse in hospitals; they
often constructed the buildings themselves.[4] They also became probation officers,
opened shelters for unwed mothers and residences for single women in the city,
and ran some of the first urban settlement houses, often over the reservations of
more traditionally-minded clergy and bishops (Fitzgerald 2006:58–59, 73–76).

This changed, however, in the twentieth century. In 1900, Pope Leo XIII's
Conditae a Christo recognized for the first time that active sisters with simple
vows were "real" religious. The implications of this new status were spelled
out the following year in restrictions that imposed partial cloister on them. In
1906, Pope Pius X established the Sacred Congregation for Religious, which was
empowered to supervise the sisters' adherence to these regulations. Then, in
1917, a new Code of Canon Law was published, and all religious communities
were ordered to revise their constitutions to conform to its prescriptions. The result, one critic has said, "was a virtual ice age" for women religious in the United
States (McNamara 1996:613). In subsequent decades, "sisters were warned to restrict contact with the outside world as much as possible. Newspapers, radios,
libraries and so on were seen as dangerous distractions, as were various kinds
of public events and meetings" (Ewens 1989:33). Habits were standardized
within congregations, and veils adopted where they had not been worn before
(Fialka 2003:162). Women religious concentrated more and more on traditional
occupations such as teaching or nursing, and less on devising creative ways to
meet the new needs that arose.

At the same time, changes were taking place in the larger secular society which
began to affect the education, health care, and social service institutions run by

---

[4] See, for example, Mother Joseph Pariseau, SP, recognized by the state of Washington for her many talents
and contributions by being named as one of the state's two representatives to the National Statuary Hall
Collection in the U.S. Capitol. Wikipedia, s.v. "Mother Joseph Pariseau," accessed Jan. 6, 2017, https://
en.wikipedia.org/wiki/Mother_Joseph_Pariseau.

both women and men religious. States began to pass laws requiring a specified level of formal education for elementary school teachers. The academies and colleges run by the sisters, brothers, and religious order priests were also being pressured to adopt a more standard high school curriculum. To meet these new educational requirements, the Third Baltimore Council encouraged the sisters' congregations to establish teachers' colleges (called "Normal Schools" in those days) for their members. While initially very rudimentary and haphazard in their curriculum, these institutions eventually became full-fledged colleges and began to admit lay women as well. Other women's congregations gradually upgraded their academies to offer college courses. Between 1900 and 1950, women religious established more than seventy colleges in the United States, and upgraded another twenty-two of their academies.

In response to the same societal changes, the "colleges" run by the male orders also changed. The younger students were separated from the older ones and high schools were created for them, while the remaining classes were conformed to the standard American higher education model for colleges. Male orders founded twenty-three new colleges and universities, and upgraded another fifty of their older-model "colleges."[5] The male orders that operated seminaries to train diocesan clergy also had to adjust their curriculum and train the members on their faculties to meet new credentialing standards.

Hospitals experienced even greater pressures. With the discovery of anesthesia and modern antiseptic techniques, hospitals shifted from merely being places where the destitute were cared for until they died to being institutions that actually cured people. As a result, more people desired treatment in them, and the sisters could no longer provide all the services for their expanding clientele. As with the educational institutions, there were also new government requirements for the credentialing of nurses. No longer was it possible for a young sister to be trained as a nurse "on the job." To meet these two new demands, the sisters began to establish nursing schools in their hospitals, to train both their own members and also the young laywomen who were needed to supplement the sisters' work. There were 403 such schools by 1931 (Wittberg 2006:32).

Sources of Vocations

Throughout the nineteenth century and the first half of the twentieth, Catholic educational institutions served as a fertile source of vocations. American bishops

---

[5] Calculated from Michael Glazier and Thomas Shelley, eds., *Encyclopedia of American Catholic History* (Collegeville, MN: Liturgical Press, 1997), 302–307.

and religious order priests founded colleges for young men at least partly in order to recruit new members to their ranks (Wittberg 2006:75). During the first half of the twentieth century, it was not unusual for 10 to 15 percent of the graduates of the sisters' academies and colleges to enter the community that had taught them (Oates 2002:172; Ebaugh 1993:95–98; Conway 2002:13). Often, in fact, *all* of an order's postulants came from its own schools.[6] Nursing schools, too, provided a steady stream of young women to the sisterhoods that staffed the hospitals. Some orders also accepted recruits from the orphanages they operated.

A second source of vocations was the Catholic families themselves. Having a son or daughter in the priesthood or religious life was a source of pride and status in many immigrant parishes, as well as an avenue of upward mobility for the young entrant himself or herself. Entering religious life offered an opportunity for an education and a spiritually fulfilling career—an opportunity that may have been otherwise unavailable to the children of the immigrant working class (Oates 1985:176). It also helped that many young women and men already had relatives in the order they were planning to enter: aunts or uncles, older sisters or brothers, cousins, even widowed parents. "Sometimes two or three natural sisters would join the same sisterhood simultaneously. Women who could count favored aunts or cousins as role models often followed them into convent life and sometimes into the same convent" (Fitzgerald 2006:32). In one Wisconsin order of sisters, over 25 percent of its four hundred members had relatives in the same community (Wittberg 1994:102–103).

Summary

By 1950, most of the religious orders and congregations in the United States had established themselves quite firmly in an institutionalized and self-replicating environment. "Their recruiting channels and their sources of support had become routinized: Pastors often erected parish schools even before the church was finished; parents dutifully sent their children there; the schools regularly funneled a proportion of their graduates into seminaries and novitiates; newly ordained or professed religious returned to teach in the schools and inspire subsequent generations to devote their lives to God. Old motherhouses, hospitals, and academies were outgrown and new ones constructed" (Wittberg 1994:209). The future seemed fixed, stable, and optimistic. After 1950, however, things changed.

---

[6] Oates (1985:176) reports that, of forty-two postulants entering the Sisters of Notre Dame in 1930, all but one came from the sisters' own schools.

CHANGES IN RELIGIOUS LIFE AFTER 1950

Religious life in the United States today appears substantially different from the 1940s. In part, this is due to changes in the Church itself and in the Church's expectations for male and female religious. In part, however, it is also due to wide-ranging external changes in the larger American society, which impacted everyone in this country. As a result of these larger changes in the Church and society, the religious orders also changed: in the number of their members, in the ministries they performed, and in the sources of their vocational recruitment.

External Impacts

Restrictive immigration laws passed in the 1920s cut off the stream of immigration to the United States. By the 1950s, therefore, most of the Catholic immigrants who had populated the encapsulated urban neighborhoods of earlier decades had aged or died, and their children and grandchildren were thoroughly assimilated to the larger American culture. This assimilation process was accelerated by common experiences among the GIs in World War II, and by the educational opportunities offered by the GI Bill after the war. Declines in anti-Catholic bias led to increased opportunities for Catholics in education, jobs, and housing. The 1950s and 1960s also witnessed the large-scale movement of Catholics out of inner-city ethnic enclaves and into the newly built suburbs. Suburban Catholic parents often did not feel the same need to send their children to parish schools, particularly when the suburban public schools were larger and better equipped. Meanwhile, inner city parishes saw the enrollment in their schools plummet as new arrivals to their neighborhoods were less likely to be Catholic. Many of these schools were ultimately forced to close. Meanwhile, the demand for college education among Catholics had greatly increased. In response to this demand, the number of Catholic colleges grew from 169 in 1945 to 224 in 1965, and the number of students attending them grew from 232,000 to 402,000 (Gleason 2001:1–19). Higher education led to middle-class jobs in the South and the West, where established Catholic enclaves often did not exist.

Health care institutions also grew in size and became more and more professionalized. Not only were religious orders unable to fill the nursing staff positions with their own members, but they increasingly found it difficult even to fill the administrative positions. Catholic hospitals hired their first lay department supervisors in the 1940s. To deal with the increasing number of lay staff and administrators, the hospitals began to form personnel departments and codify their labor policies. These trends accelerated in subsequent decades.

By the 1960s and 1970s, many orders were unable even to provide sisters for the top positions in their hospitals. In 1965 only 3 percent of the top administrative positions in Catholic hospitals were filled by lay administrators; this percentage rose to 23 percent in 1970, to 70 percent in 1985, and to over 90 percent by the year 2000 (Wittberg 2006:128). The hiring standards for filling these positions were increasingly modeled on mainstream secular standards: An order could no longer be sure, even if one of its members earned a degree in hospital administration, that he or she would be hired in its own hospital (Wittberg 2006:216–217). Another change, the rise of third-party payers such as Blue Cross and (later) Medicare, necessitated more formal billing and accounting procedures as well as conformity to government- and insurance-mandated standards of care. Similar conformity to secular standards of professionalization and bureaucratization occurred in the orders' social service institutions, and in their colleges or universities. The operational standardization mandated by governments and professional organizations rendered the orders' schools, hospitals, and social service agencies less distinctive. It became hard to tell exactly what made these organizations specifically "Franciscan," "Jesuit," or "Mercy"—or even what made them specifically "Catholic."

Finally, there was an increase in the types of work that were open to young Catholics in the larger society. No longer was religious life the only option for a young man or woman to receive an education or to develop skills and talents in God's service. Between 1970 and 2000, the percentage of women in the labor force grew from 43.3 percent to 60.2 percent (Information Please 2016). A young woman graduating from high school was aware that there were many more opportunities open to her than to her mother or grandmother. At the same time, the Women's Movement exposed women and girls to occupations and institutions that discriminated against them.

Changes within Religious Life

Religious life, too, was changing. It may surprise most Catholics to learn that these changes did not begin with the second Vatican Council. As early as 1950, Pope Pius XII had worried about the decline in vocations to women's religious congregations which he saw occurring in Europe after World War II. The Pope believed that this was because young women were put off by the overly strict and obsolete customs of women's religious orders, and by their lack of up-to-date professional education. With his encouragement, the Sacred Congregation for Religious convened its first General Assembly of Religious in the fall of 1950. Some four thousand superiors of religious orders attended. In his address to the Assembly, the Pope urged them to adapt their "excessively strict" and outdated cloister restrictions and to reduce whatever archaic and nonessential customs were hindering their apostolates (Wittberg 1994:210). The Pope also urged the sisters to spare no expense in providing the best professional education to equip their young members for ministry: "This is important for your sisters' peace and for their work" (Wittberg 1994:211).

In response to the Pope's request, the women's communities in the United States established the Sister Formation Conference in 1952, to promote the professional and theological training of their members. In 1956, again because of direct prodding from the Vatican, the heads of both the men's and the women's communities established two umbrella organizations, the Conference of Major Superiors of Men (CMSM) and the Conference of Major Superiors of Women (CMSW). These groups began to work for the creation of "Juniorates" where newly-professed sisters and brothers might remain to complete their degrees before being sent to a ministry. Progress was slow, however, since the pressure to provide schooling for the Catholic children of the post-war Baby Boom was so intense. Also, many of the orders, especially women's congregations, did not have the funds to send all of their young sisters to colleges and universities to study. Still, however, these early developments sensitized the members of religious congregations to the need for changes and updating.

On October 11, 1962, the recently-elected Pope John XXIII opened the Second Vatican Council. It is impossible to overstate the impact the Council had on religious life, both in the United States and in the entire world. In the first place, its primary document on the Church, *Lumen Gentium*, declared that all members of the Church were equally called to holiness. This implied that vowed religious life was not a holier state than that of laypeople. A second document, "The Church in the Modern World" (*Gaudium et Spes*), called on all Catholics to become more involved in the larger society. This seemed contrary to earlier expectations that religious should be cloistered and separated from the world. Some observers even thought that these two documents had made religious life obsolete.

The Conciliar and post-Conciliar documents gave mixed signals as to exactly how religious orders were to respond to them: On the one hand, the Council called for the orders to return to the entrepreneurial spirit of their founders and early members; on the other hand, the post-Conciliar decree *Perfectae Caritatis* (1965) and subsequent documents such as the "Essential Elements" of religious life (1983) continued to assume a more traditional model. The resulting confusion led to discord, especially among women religious: Between 1970 and 1971, the more conservative women's congregations withdrew from CMSW (which had recently changed its name to the Leadership Conference of Women Religious, or LCWR, because the idea of "Major Superiors" was thought to be too elitist), and organized their own umbrella group. In 1992, this second group, the Council of Major Superiors of Women Religious (CMSWR) was also recognized by the Vatican. The United States, therefore, is the only country in the world with two different associations representing women religious: the LCWR and the CMSWR.

Ministry Changes

Called by the Second Vatican Council to return to the spirit and charism of their founders, many sisters, brothers, and religious order priests moved into new areas of ministry among the poor. In addition, as their traditional education and health care ministries expanded and professionalized, many orders were less able to staff them. In the 1940s and 1950s, the faculties at most Catholic colleges had been less than 30 or 40 percent lay; by the 1990s, over 95 percent were laity. On average, only 4 percent of the faculty at Jesuit universities were Jesuits in 1998, and only 3 percent of the faculty at Notre Dame were members of the sponsoring Holy Cross order (Wittberg 2006:118–119). Fewer and fewer religious taught in Catholic elementary and high schools either. Many Catholic hospitals had merged into large health care systems by the 1990s, and over 90 percent of these hospitals' and systems' CEOs were not members of a religious order. Neither were hardly any of the nurses, technicians, and other personnel who worked in them.

These changes in ministry affected the religious orders in several ways. One was in the ability of the members to live a communal life style. In the new ministries to which the male and female religious moved, there were few living arrangements that could accommodate five or ten adults. Unless their order owned such a residence, religious often found themselves with only one- or two-bedroom apartments in the mainstream housing market to choose from. As early as 1982, 10 percent of sisters were living alone, or with only one or two others, in rented apartments or houses. This was a pronounced departure from 1968, when almost all had resided in convents housing larger communities (Wittberg 1994:254). By the end of the century, 69 percent of active sisters (i.e., those not in their order's retirement home) lived alone or in groups of two, despite the fact that most preferred living in a larger community (Wittberg 2006:188). These small-scale living arrangements provided "no room for guests, potential new members, or even one's own community members. There is no room for a common prayer space, and no room to welcome groups of guests" (Wittberg 2006:188) When a group of male or female religious *was* able to find a larger residence that would house more people, the varied ministerial schedules of the residents often hindered communal bonding and support systems.

Vocational Recruitment

Another impact of the changes in ministry was a loss of the former channels by which new members had been recruited to the orders. Without the presence of religious in their schools, which had been such a fertile source of vocations in the past, young men and women had fewer opportunities to get to know sisters, brothers, and religious order priests and to become acquainted with their lives. Jesuit high schools in the 1960s generally had a dozen young Jesuit scholastics teaching in the school, but by 1990 there would be only one scholastic, or none, teaching in each of the 50 Jesuit high schools across the nation. Additionally, as religious aged and their numbers shrank, fewer young people could say they had relatives in religious life. Deprived of personal contact with them, young adults often formed their impression of religious from movies and news stories, sources which were often inaccurate or off-putting (Sabine 2013).

The conflicting messages about religious life that followed the Second Vatican Council also affected vocational recruitment. A study of men and women religious conducted in 1990 found that barely half of the sisters surveyed scored "high" on a measurement of role clarity, as did barely two-thirds of brothers and religious order priests (Nygren and Ukeritis 1993:190). This led to a growing reluctance to invite new members. After the Council, religious life was no longer viewed, either by families or by the religious themselves, as a "higher calling." Nor was it seen as a way out of a working class life for those with limited resources. Still another difficulty stemmed from the decreasing size of families. Parents with only one or two children tended to be more reluctant to have one of them enter religious life. As Chapter 2 will show, these various external changes in the larger society, and the internal changes experienced by the religious orders themselves, have all contributed to a decline in the number of sisters, brothers, and religious order priests ministering in the United States today.

THE PLAN OF THIS BOOK

By the end of the twentieth century, religious life in the United States had experienced over thirty years of rapid and sometimes disorienting change following Vatican II. Many members expressed a profound appreciation for the opportunities for spiritual and intellectual growth which the post-Vatican II renewal of religious life had brought about, and many gave inspiring service in their new ministries to the poor and marginalized of society. But as their previous sources of new members diminished, many also began to feel that the future of their own institute was in jeopardy. An influential national study of men and women religious conducted in the early 1990s warned that many orders had only a ten- to fifteen-year window of opportunity to revise their community life and ministries and to attract a new generation of members before the likelihood of their survival would become extremely precarious (Nygren and Ukeritis 1993:229–251).

The window of opportunity postulated by the study cited above is now long past. What is the state of religious life in the United States today? Which institutes are increasing in number, and which are decreasing or ceasing to exist? From what ethnic and socioeconomic populations are they drawing their members? What new religious institutes and ecclesial movements are being founded and how successful are they? Which of their traditional ministries continue to be staffed and administered by religious, and what new ministries have been undertaken? What influences a young man or woman to consider religious life today? How many religious from other countries are coming to the United States to minister today and what difficulties and opportunities do they face?

The present book addresses many of these questions, using data from the many studies of religious life in the United States that CARA has conducted over the last ten years. Chapter 2 will present the long view, describing population trends among religious institutes since 1970 and charting which orders have experienced sharp decreases in membership, which have decreased only slightly, and which have actually increased. The next block of chapters will summarize recent CARA studies on the various factors that influence religious vocations: Chapter 3 will summarize the studies of families and their influence on religious vocations. Chapter 4 will summarize CARA research on the educational experience of religious, before and after their entrance into religious life. Chapter 5 will explore CARA's studies of how the increasing number of Catholic volunteer programs has influenced religious vocations, while Chapter 6 will look at other influences on vocations, such as prior ministry engagement and parish activities.

The next block of chapters will summarize CARA research on some of the emerging trends in religious life in the United States. Chapter 7 will describe the emergence of lay associates in religious institutes. Chapter 8 will summarize the findings of CARA's three directories of emerging religious institutes and lay ecclesial movements. Published in 1999, 2006, and 2017, an examination of these three directories reveals trends in the number and type of religious institutes founded in the United States since the Second Vatican Council. Chapter 9 will discuss another new trend in religious life in the United States: the number of sisters and priests studying and ministering here who come from other countries. Finally, Chapter 10 will offer recommendations from these findings for religious orders and vocation directors who wish to attract new members in the future.

2

Population Trends among Religious Institutes since 1970

Mary L. Gautier

⌒──

WHILE THE LAST chapter examined the dramatic growth in numbers of men and women religious in the United States by the middle of the twentieth century, this chapter explores in some detail the downward trend in numbers that these groups have experienced since that time. In this chapter we disentangle the patterns of variation among religious institutes that is hidden within an overall narrative of decline. Past studies that have presented the overall population of Catholic vowed religious in the United States focused on the rapid decline since the late 1960s, but such studies did not provide the more nuanced narrative of what decline meant for the individual religious institute. How, for example, did religious institutes respond to declining membership? *The Official Catholic Directory* (OCD), published annually since 1899, lists the numbers in each religious institute for each year. Our exploration of the data reveal not one response, but quite varied responses among particular religious institutes. We explore the population trends among religious institutes of women first. Later in the chapter we present a similar analysis of the population trends among religious institutes of men. Finally, we end the chapter with a presentation of some of the demographic characteristics of the members of these institutes.

TRENDS AMONG RELIGIOUS INSTITUTES OF WOMEN

Lost in the discussion of the overall decline in numbers of women religious since the late 1960s are the stories of religious institutes that have not followed the trend.[1] Religious institutes experiencing some growth, for instance, were virtually unaccounted for in past studies. Since the total growth in vocations did not surpass the number needed for replacement, many institutes were assumed to have no new members, which is not the case. While new vocations to religious life are not abundant at this time, it is important to recognize that women continue to be called to this way of life. Although the numbers overall continue to decline, this chapter presents signs of life that are hidden in those numbers. The religious institutes discussed here were selected by following trends in the collected data.[2] Following the data allows us to investigate why some institutes declined at a lower rate than others and to see the growth in some institutes. Why did some institutes of women religious defy the general trend over time, while others closely mirrored it?

General Observations among Religious Institutes of Women

The overall pattern of change in the population of women religious in the United States over the past 45 years is one of dramatic and well-documented decline. As was described in the previous chapter, the overall population of women religious in the United States grew rapidly over the course of the twentieth century and reached its peak in 1965 with 181,421 sisters. Presently, the total number of women religious serving in the United States has fallen below 50,000—representing a 72.5-percent decline from the peak in 1965. There are about as many women religious in the United States now as there were a hundred years ago.

While many have lamented the decline and some have speculated as to its causes and implications, few have actually examined the trend lines for the individual

---

[1] We thank Erick Berrelleza, SJ, for compiling the data in this section and writing a CARA Special Report of the findings, titled *Population Trends among Religious Institutes of Women*.

[2] For this analysis, CARA compiled data on the total number of sisters reported to the OCD by each institute of women religious in 1970, 1980, 1990, 2000, 2010, and 2014 (the most recent edition available at the time of data collection). To compare growth or decline over time, CARA calculated the slope of the trend line for all institutes with data across all six years. A positive slope indicates overall growth between 1970 and 2013, while a negative slope indicates overall decline across that same period. Of the 492 units for which a slope could be calculated, 444 showed a negative slope and 48 showed a positive slope. Anomalous data trends, such as religious institutes that did not follow the general pattern observed in other communities, led to further research that uncovered the unusual patterns described in this chapter. Researching an institute's history enabled CARA to fill in the narrative hidden in the numbers and to identify orders that disappeared in later editions of the OCD.

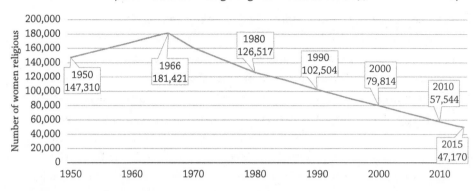

FIGURE 2.1. Total Numbers of Sisters in the United States
Source: The Official Catholic Directory (relevant years).

institutes of women religious as this chapter does. A number of stories in the popular press have made the claim that the more traditionalist institutes (e.g., those where the women wear a full traditional habit) are growing, while those institutes where they do not wear a traditional habit are declining. However, as Johnson, Wittberg, and Gautier report, "The reality of the situation is that an almost equal percentage of LCWR [Leadership Conference of Women Religious] and CMSWR [Conference of Major Superiors of Women Religious] institutes have no one at all in formation at the present time (32 percent and 27 percent, respectively). One of the most striking findings regarding new entrants is that almost equal numbers of women have been attracted to institutes in both conferences in recent years" (2014:20–21). The reality that the data from the OCD disclose is that nine in ten institutes follow the trend line shown in Figure 2.1 while one in ten have slowed or even reversed that trend.

The largest religious institute of women in the United States remains the Sisters of Mercy of the Americas, with just over 3,000 members in 2015. In 1970, the OCD listed nearly 13,000 Sisters of Mercy. This institute was founded in 1991, when nine provinces and sixteen congregations of Sisters of Mercy came together. These twenty-five later consolidated into five U.S. provinces and one Latin American province. This institute illustrates the general pattern of decline and merger found in most institutes.

Pattern 1: Explaining Sharp Declines

A few religious institutes of women stood out in the data, displaying rapid rates of decline over a short period of time. An investigation of these institutes reveals that these sharp declines in membership occurred shortly after the Second Vatican Council (1962–1965), which coincided with a period of turmoil and rapid social change in the United States. The Council had called for *aggiornamento*— or "bringing up to date"—which left many religious orders with the task of determining what updating might mean for their particular institute. Renewal proved especially difficult, however, because the Council had, at the same time, called for what was termed *ressourcement*—or a renewal through a return to the sources. These two calls could be seen as complementing, or as conflicting with, each other. For many sisters, looking back to their initial foundation and charism suggested ways to read the "signs of the times," which facilitated renewal of their institutes. For others, debates ensued that caused irreconcilable divisions. Some sisters responded by breaking from their institutes in order to found new religious institutes, while others sought dispensation from their vows altogether.

A well-known example of mass exodus in an institute's history is found in The California Institute of the Sisters of the Most Holy and Immaculate Heart of the Blessed Virgin Mary (Figure 2.2). In the period following Vatican II, these women determined what the Council's call for *aggiornamento* would mean for their Los Angeles-based institute. Cardinal McIntyre, Archbishop of Los Angeles, vehemently disagreed with a number of changes in their institute and barred the sisters from teaching in diocesan schools when they refused to comply with his wishes. The confrontation with Cardinal McIntyre caused a rift within the religious institute, with some members desiring to comply while the vast majority maintained that these changes were needed.

The Vatican commission sent to investigate the dispute concluded its investigation with a compromise that allowed the community to split temporarily and continue their discussions. At the time, fifty sisters remained in the original

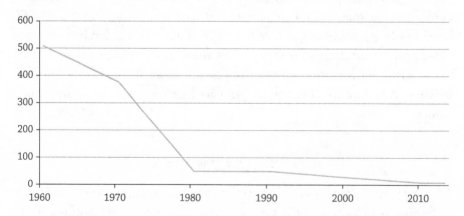

FIGURE 2.2. The California Institute of the Sisters of the Most Holy and Immaculate Heart of the Blessed Virgin Mary

Source: The Official Catholic Directory (relevant years).

institute. Unable to reach an agreement, the other 300 plus members of the institute sought dispensation from their canonical vows in favor of a lay movement called the Immaculate Heart Community. *Time* magazine called them "rebels," but these were simply women grappling with Vatican II's call for *aggiornamento*.

Pattern 2: Internal Reorganization of Existing Religious Institutes

An examination of data reported to the OCD reveals several religious institutes of women that did not follow the general trend of rapid and increasing rate of decline. A number of religious institutes stood out in the data by evidencing a slowing decline rate since 2000. However, when these communities with slowing rates of diminishment were investigated further, a number of them were found to have absorbed smaller communities (or institutes with a much higher rate of population decrease) thereby accounting for the slowing decline trend in the base community.

The Sisters of St. Joseph of Springfield (in Holyoke, Massachusetts) is one helpful example (Figure 2.3). In the mid-1970s, the Sisters of St. Joseph of Springfield accepted the Sisters of St. Joseph of Fall River into their institute. Prior to joining the Springfield institute in 1974, the Fall River institute had numbered ninety-nine sisters. With their inclusion, in 1975 the Springfield institute's membership increased by ninety-nine members. In 2001, the Sisters of St. Joseph of Rutland, Vermont, likewise joined the Sisters of St. Joseph of Springfield. The addition of these two institutes to the institute in Holyoke, Massachusetts, helps to explain the increase in the numbers for the institute in 1974 and 2001. It is not that the Sisters of St. Joseph of Springfield exhibited a sudden increase in new

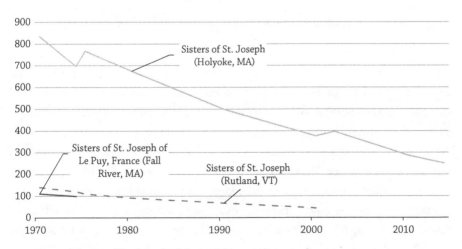

FIGURE 2.3. Sisters of St. Joseph of Springfield
Source: The Official Catholic Directory (relevant years).

vocations, but rather adding these two smaller institutes accounted for the up-swing. In such cases, the slowing rate of decline does not seem to be related to an increase in new members.

Other larger institutes have reorganized internally, or are in the process of reorganizing, by reshaping their province jurisdictions. In some cases, this entails returning to an organizational model once employed in their earlier history. Such religious institutes deal with decline in members internally, rather than through merger with another religious institute. In the past, a rapidly growing institute would have responded to increased numbers by creating new provinces in order to better administer their religious community. Today, faced with a corresponding rapid decline, such an institute might consolidate provinces to form fewer, larger provinces and do away with replicated administration offices across the country. By responding in this internal manner, a religious institute might avoid the challenges of merging with another institute that may not share its charism and traditions.

The Daughters of Charity of St. Vincent de Paul, for example, were founded as the Sisters of Charity of St. Joseph at Emmitsburg, Maryland, in 1809 and di-vided into two provinces in 1910 (the St. Louis Province and the Eastern Province). In 1960, those two provinces reported more than 2,500 total members. A short time later (ca. 1969), the organizational structure for the institute swelled to five U.S. provinces to respond to growth in numbers of sisters. In 2011, however, the St. Louise Province was established, which joined together four of the five prov-inces and thereby returned to the previous organizational model of the institute. Today, the Daughters of Charity of St. Vincent de Paul list 670 members serving in the United States.

Pattern 3: New Religious Institutes Merged from Previously Existing Ones

The formation of "new" religious institutes, amalgamated from smaller commu-nities of women, is a common trend among religious institutes faced with declining numbers. This pattern is different from the internal reorganization described above in that the communities that merge into a new religious institute were never part of the same institute. They do not share a common founder or foundress; they may not even share a common charism. This reorganization of communities explains why a number of religious institutes cease to exist while other institutes, often larger than 500 members, have suddenly appeared in more recent years. It is not that communities have vanished, but simply that they are to be found under new designations. The Sisters of St. Francis of the Neumann Communities, for example, is the result of a merger of five communities beginning in 2004. The five communities varied in size from 30 to 335 members. After the merger, the new institute known as Sisters of St. Francis of the Neumann Communities numbered 528 members in 2010.

Many other institutes of women religious will reorganize or merge institutes as numbers continue to decline. Recently, the Union of Sisters of Our Lady of Charity celebrated their reunification with the Religious of the Good Shepherd. The amalgamation of these two institutes represents an international merger, bringing together traditions and resources under a shared charism. Transition marks the experience of many sisters, as they work to negotiate their past with hopes for the future.

Pattern 4: Communities with Vocational Growth

Although the overall trend among religious institutes today is downward, some institutes with established histories continue to experience vocational success. The Dominican Sisters of the Congregation of St. Cecilia (also known as the Nashville Dominicans) is one such example (Figure 2.4).

Following a slight decline between 1970 and 1980, the Congregation of St. Cecilia has since steadily grown. The institute experienced its most rapid growth in the period since 2000, with a 76-percent increase during that time. Today, the community numbers about 300 members and new members continue to join their ranks. Growth, not decline, captures this institute's trajectory.

The CARA studies of emerging communities of consecrated life,[3] reported in greater detail in Chapter 8, below, reveal that a number of new communities, many of which were founded in the 1970s, display a period of initial success followed by the more common pattern of decline. These religious institutes, inspired by the Second Vatican Council, placed themselves at the service of the Church with a renewed commitment to the poor. The Sisters of St. Joseph the Worker, for example, were founded in 1973 in the Diocese of Covington, Kentucky, by sisters from the Sisters of Charity of Nazareth. They began with eighteen professed sisters and experienced growth in the early years of their foundation. Their apostolic life was dedicated to the care of the elderly and the education of children at their academy in Walton, Kentucky. By 1990, the community numbered twenty-three sisters, representing a growth of 27 percent since 1973. The years following, however, returned the Sisters of St. Joseph the Worker to a size comparable to that of their initial foundation. Today, the community numbers twelve members, a decline of 48 percent from 1990.

---

[3] Patricia A. Wittberg, SC, and Mary L. Gautier, eds., *Emerging U.S. Communities of Consecrated Life since Vatican II* (Washington, DC: Center for Applied Research in the Apostolate, 2017).

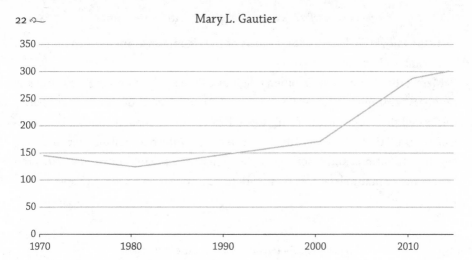

FIGURE 2.4. Dominican Sisters of the Congregation of St. Cecilia
Source: The Official Catholic Directory (relevant years).

A few other religious institutes of women that emerged in the 1970s experience consistent growth and seem to point to even further expansion in the foreseeable future. Established in 1973 with only nine members, the Sisters of Mercy of Alma, Michigan, serve as such an example of ongoing growth. Currently, they have eighty-three full members. If their vocational success continues with at least the same vitality, the community will exceed one hundred members by the end of the decade.

CARA's analysis of the OCD data identified six religious institutes of women that have doubled their membership between 1970 and 2013. Some of these units are cited in anecdotes and news reports as evidence of a reversal in this overall trend of diminishment. However, all six institutes together have increased their net membership by only 267 members since 1970, too few to have an effect on the overall picture. Whatever these institutes have done or are doing is unlikely to offset losses in the tens of thousands elsewhere. It is simply not enough.

Pattern 5: International Institutes

Many religious institutes of women in the United States are simply one part of an international order. The U.S. provinces of these communities therefore do not provide the full picture of the story. In some cases, the U.S. branch of the institute represents just a small delegation of the international order and might furthermore be composed of members who are born and formed abroad. Decline for these communities inevitably means an honest appraisal of the situation in the United States and a response situated in a global context. At times such an appraisal will lead to the withdrawal of the members serving in the United States to a ministry deemed to be in greater need of support internationally. Other communities might respond to aging and decline of membership in the United States by sending more sisters from another part of the world. An international religious institute might, for example, send sisters from their congregation in India to minister in the United States, where apostolates may continue to thrive but whose membership is low. Further investigation of international sisters will be discussed in Chapter 9, below.

The Irish Ursulines of Blackrock, having a prominent history of missionary work, established a new mission in the United States in the 1960s with a small delegation of women. The sisters arrived in Georgia, ministering in the Diocese of Savannah until they approached the age of retirement. Vocations do not appear to have boomed in their mission territory, since the numbers of sisters in the U.S. delegation remained relatively consistent over the reported years. The remaining sisters in the United States (four in number) returned to Ireland in 1997, rejoining the larger contingent of women from their religious institute. This decision marked the cessation of direct missionary activity in the United States. Advanced age (and likely declining numbers in Ireland) influenced the decision of this institute to return to its home foundation.

Another notable phenomenon is found in the Sisters of Charity of Seton Hill (Greensburg, Pennsylvania). Originally established in the United States in 1870 with only three sisters and two novices from the Sisters of Charity of Cincinnati community, the Sisters of Charity of Seton Hill enjoyed vocational success in the Diocese of Pittsburgh. Only nineteen years after the first sisters moved to the Pittsburgh area, the Seton Hill sisters were staffing twenty parochial schools as well as their own flagship schools, Saint Mary School for Boys and Saint Joseph Academy for Girls. By

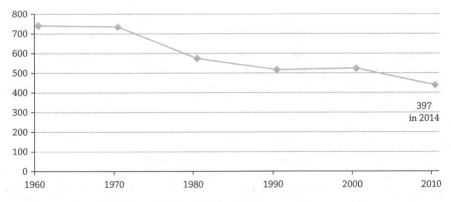

FIGURE 2.5. Sisters of Charity of Seton Hill (Total Sisters)
Source: The Official Catholic Directory (relevant years).

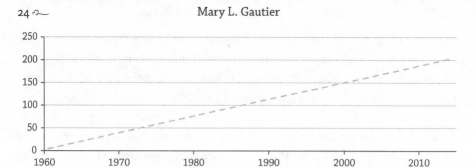

FIGURE 2.6. Sisters of Charity of Seton Hill (Sisters Ministering in South Korea)
Note: Trend line denotes the approximate number of sisters working in South Korea.
Source: The Official Catholic Directory (relevant years).

1960, the Sisters of Charity of Seton Hill numbered 741 sisters in the United States (Figure 2.5). That same year, the institute set its eyes on the missions by electing to send four sisters to South Korea at the invitation of a bishop.

Lost in the presentation of raw figures of total sisters for this religious institute, however, is the overwhelming growth experienced in the international mission. The rate of decline of this religious institute has been slowed by the continuing vocational vitality in South Korea. In one way, the number of sisters reported by the Sisters of Charity of Seton Hill inflates the number found in the U.S. community. For many OCD entries, the Sisters of Charity of Seton Hill did not distinguish the South Korean sisters from the U.S.-based sisters, but rather provided only a total number of sisters in the religious institute. However, the example proves useful in drawing attention to the rapid growth of international sisters for this community (Figure 2.6).

The original U.S. foundation experiences a steady decline similar to other religious institutes of its size. Today, more than half of the sisters belonging to the Sisters of Charity of Seton Hill are ministering in South Korea. In the case of the Sisters of Charity of Seton Hill, therefore, the mission territory experienced a more robust growth in vocations than its original U.S. foundation. The story of vocational strength of this religious institute has flipped. While several of the members of the Korean Province of the Sisters of Charity of Seton Hill are American-born, most of the sisters serving in Korea are native to that country. Perhaps one day, the United States will itself become the mission territory of this religious institute with sisters coming from South Korea to minister here.

Pattern 6: Defunct/Extinct Institutes

For a number of institutes, data were only available for the 1970 reporting cycle and did not appear in later editions of the OCD. Accounting for these institutes led to an investigation of defunct communities. After determining that these institutes had not merged with another group, CARA looked for the historical trajectory of these unamalgamated and now defunct diocesan communities.

The Society of Christ Our King, for example, began in 1931 in the Diocese of Raleigh and moved to Danville, Virginia, in 1938. Under the guidance of a Carmelite nun from Philadelphia, the community established itself in social outreach at local parishes. Gaining national attention in 1951 for their Hattie Carnegie-designed habit, the hard-working sisters were praised by *Time* magazine for their modern dress. The early 1960s presented a further refinement in apostolic outreach for the sisters. With civil rights demonstrations mounting in the area and instruction from the local bishop to refrain from public demonstrations themselves, the sisters opted to provide hospitality to demonstrators at their convent (Moore 2006). There are conflicting accounts as to why the community was eventually disbanded, but one author suggests the possibility that the Society of Christ Our King had never gained canonical recognition as a religious institute (Fogarty 2001). Never growing beyond ten members, the Society of Christ Our King dissolved in the early 1970s.

Today, there are fewer religious institutes of women based in the United States than there were in the 1970s, but determining an accurate number of institutes for any given year is really a matter of semantics. In one accounting, a number for religious communities could include the number of provinces of a single religious institute. Such a count would grossly overestimate the number of total institutes but would account for the changes in internal structures. Another accounting could exclude the individual provinces but this would grossly underestimate some religious communities with distinct foundations.

TRENDS AMONG RELIGIOUS INSTITUTES OF MEN[4]

We now turn to population trends in the number of men religious, as reported by the OCD. To examine these trends, we created seven categories that are based on observation of the trends among the various institutes within this overall population. The first three categories present the ten largest institutes, the ten institutes surrounding the median (the midpoint of all religious institutes as ranked by size), and the ten smallest institutes according to the number of members listed in the OCD in 1970. A fourth category is new religious institutes that were not listed in 1970.[5] The fifth category analyzes the trends of the few institutes that displayed

---

[4] We thank Santiago Sordo Palacios for compiling the data presented in this section and writing a CARA Special Report of the findings, titled *Population Trends among Religious Institutes of Men*.

[5] A significant number of institutes were either founded or came to the United States after 1970. Since these institutes had a membership of zero in 1970, the analysis of overall trends would have been skewed by their presence. As a result, CARA researchers treated them in a separate category.

growth during the years studied. The final two categories consist of observations of brother-only institutes and monastic institutes, respectively.[6]

General Observations among Religious Institutes of Men

Unlike the majority of religious institutes of women, most religious institutes of men are international, meaning that they were founded outside the United States. These international institutes have a Generalate outside the United States and one or more U.S. provinces or regional bodies. To some extent, their international character insulates them from the effects of vocational decline in any one country. For the purposes of this chapter, we restrict our analysis to the numbers in their U.S. provinces or regions, just as we have done with the international religious institutes of women.

Similar to the trend among women's institutes, total membership among U.S. religious institutes of men has decreased dramatically across the last forty-five years, from almost 42,000 in 1970 to fewer than 18,000 in 2015, a decline of 58 percent (Figure 2.7). This drop is especially significant given the growing Catholic population in the United States, which has increased from 47,900,000 in 1970 to 68,100,000 in 2015.

While the number of men in religious institutes has declined over the past forty-five years, the number of religious institutes of men that are listed in *The Official Catholic Directory* has actually increased. In 1970 there were 116 institutes listed; in 2015 there were 131 institutes. Twenty-four institutes that were not listed in 1970 are included in the 2015 OCD and nine institutes that were listed in 1970 are no longer included in 2015.

There are fourteen religious institutes that reported growth in members during this period, increasing from 640 members to 1,227 members among these fourteen institutes. In addition, there are twenty-four institutes that either did not have a presence in the United States in 1970 or came into existence since 1970. These twenty-four institutes, reporting a combined total of 896 members in 2015, are examined later in this chapter.[7]

---

[6] The OCD contains a list of Religious Institutes of Brothers, which was used to identify the institutes that we classify as brother-only. CARA consulted the Conference of Major Superiors of Men for a list of monastic institutes.

[7] CARA worked diligently to ensure accurate figures for the membership of each religious institute. It is possible, however, that some religious institutes exist in the United States that either are not listed in the OCD or elect not to provide their numbers to OCD. Nevertheless, *The Official Catholic Directory* is the most comprehensive listing of religious institutes of men in the United States, and the data provided therein are the most reliable data available for this study.

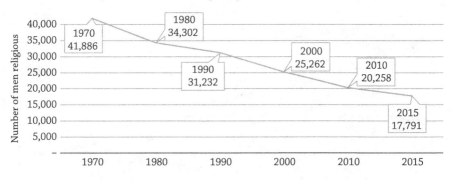

FIGURE 2.7. Membership in Religious Institutes of Men
Source: The Official Catholic Directory (relevant years).

The size of religious institutes of men vary greatly. There are many institutes with fewer than fifty members as well as a handful of institutes with more than a thousand U.S. members. In 1970, there were forty-two institutes with fifty or fewer members and ten institutes with more than a thousand men. In 2015, there were sixty-eight institutes with fifty or fewer men and only three institutes with more than a thousand men. The median size of a religious institute of men in 1970 was 109; in 2015 the median size was 40. This means that more than half of the religious institutes of men in the United States now have fewer than fifty members. Because the difference in membership size is so great among religious institutes, their membership trends are next examined here according to three categories of institute size in 1970: the ten largest institutes, the ten institutes surrounding the median, and the ten smallest institutes.

Largest Religious Institutes of Men

The ten largest religious institutes of men in the United States in 1970 contained 57 percent (or 22,597 members) of the total population in men's religious institutes, which was 41,886 men (Figure 2.8). The largest among them was the Society of Jesus, with 7,628 members. Still the largest, Jesuits have just over 2,300 members in 2015. Known as a leader in education, the Society of Jesus sponsors Fordham University, Georgetown University, Boston College, and 25 other colleges and universities.

Perhaps as a result of their various ministries, their international presence, or their sizable presence in the United States, seven of the ten largest institutes in 1970 are still among the seven largest institutes in 2015. However, the largest institutes' share of the total number of men in religious life has declined throughout this period. As previously noted, the ten largest institutes contained 57 percent of

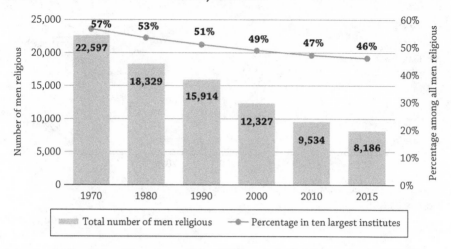

FIGURE 2.8. Number and Percentage of Men Religious in the Ten Largest Institutes of Men
Source: The Official Catholic Directory (relevant years).

the total population of men religious in 1970, but by 2015 those same institutes contained 46 percent of all men religious. As a group, the decline in membership among the ten largest institutes was steeper than the overall average across all religious institutes of men over the past 45 years.

Religious Institutes Surrounding the Median

The next category according to size includes the ten religious institutes that surround the median. In 1970, the median size among all religious institutes of men was 109 members. These institutes represented the 53rd to 64th largest institutes in the United States in 1970 and included groups such as the Missionaries of the Sacred Heart, the Brothers of Christian Instruction and the Glenmary Home Missioners. These ten institutes, unlike the ten largest, maintained a fairly steady share of the total population of men religious between 1970 and 2015. Among these ten institutes, their share of the total population of male religious was 2.9 percent in 1970 and 2.4 percent in 2015 (Figure 2.9).

Smallest Religious Institutes

This category includes the ten smallest institutes according to membership reported in 1970. Although they ranged in size from twelve to three, several of these institutes exhibited peculiar trends of growth. Unlike the trends seen in the largest and median size institutes, some of these smaller institutes—such as the Missionaries of the Holy Spirit, the Order of Our Lady of Mercy, and the Order of

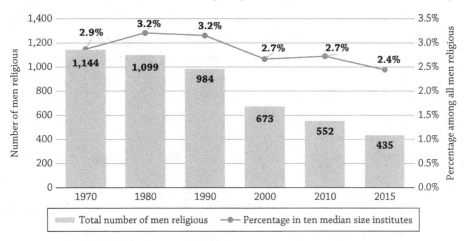

FIGURE 2.9. Number and Percentage of Men Religious in the Ten Institutes of Men Surrounding the Median
Source: The Official Catholic Directory (relevant years).

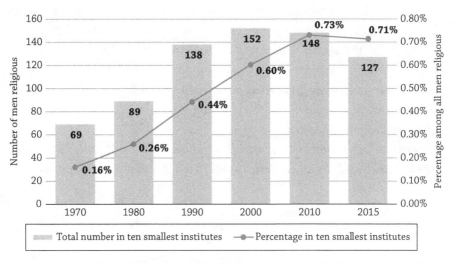

FIGURE 2.10. Number and Percentage of Men Religious in the Ten Smallest Institutes of Men
Source: The Official Catholic Directory (relevant years).

Carthusians—were among the handful that actually increased membership over the period studied. The ten smallest religious institutes increased overall in their percentage share of the total number of men in religious institutes over the forty-five years studied (Figure 2.10). In 1970, these institutes contained 0.16 percent of the total membership in religious institutes of men. By 2015, they had grown to 0.71 percent of the total membership. Although their increase is not numerically high, it is notable insofar as it represents a 344-percent increase from their original share of the total membership.

Six of the ten institutes in the smallest category experienced a significant growth over the period studied. One institute fluctuated, but in the end held the same membership—an accomplishment, given the overall decrease among men religious. The other three institutes decreased in membership. These institutes may have grown largely as a function of their very small size. When an institute is small, it often has a very clearly defined charism that can attract new vocations. It is also the case, mathematically, that it is much easier for a small community of two or three to double in size than it is for a larger community of twenty or thirty to do so.

New Religious Institutes

This category refers to religious institutes of men that either established foundations in the United States, were newly founded in the United States, or began reporting their numbers to *The Official Catholic Directory* after 1970. The groups that appear in this category are mostly small in size, and the percentage change in their reported membership over the period studied varied greatly. Figure 2.11 displays the total number of new institutes reported for each time period along with the average size among all new institutes of men.

Half of these new institutes experienced some growth between the point at which they began reporting their membership to OCD and 2015. Two others maintained the same size across the reporting period, and the rest decreased in membership over this period.

As expected, the percentage share among all religious institutes of men in the United States increased for these institutes that began reporting members in the

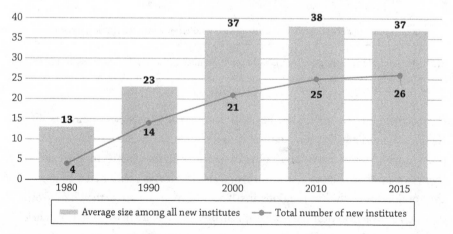

FIGURE 2.11. Average Size and Total Count of New Religious Institutes of Men
Source: The Official Catholic Directory (relevant years).

United States after 1970. These religious institutes of men that began reporting members after 1970—especially those institutes from outside the United States that established a new presence in the United States—helped to slow somewhat the rapidly declining number of priests and brothers in religious life by adding their own numbers to the existing religious institutes of men in the United States.

Only two of these new institutes had more than forty members and continually increased in size at each time period, and both of these originated in other countries before initiating their ministry in the United States. The Carmelites of Mary Immaculate began in India in 1855 and did not establish a presence in the United States until the 1980s. It reported 38 members in the United States in 1990 and had grown to 109 in 2015. The other larger new institute is the Missionary Society of St. Paul of Nigeria, founded in 1978 in Nigeria. It sent its first members to the United States in 1986. In 2000 it listed 20 members in the United States and had grown to 49 in 2015.

Other Institutes with Growing Membership

There are thirteen other religious institutes of men listed in OCD that have increased their membership between 1970 and 2015 (excluding institutes that were first listed after 1970, which were described above). These thirteen institutes have added 587 members, or an increase of 93 percent, from 631 to 1,218 members. Almost two-thirds of this increase belongs to the Legionaries of Christ, which went from 28 members in the United States to 396 members over the forty-five years. The Piarist Fathers, Society of Christ, and the Missionaries of the Holy Spirit each added thirty to forty-eight members over the same period of time, and have drawn many of their members from outside of the United States.

Brother-Only Religious Institutes

The United States is currently home to nineteen religious institutes that are exclusively lay brothers. Their ministries are focused in such a way that they are not engaged in sacramental ministry. A few of these institutes have a handful of priests that serve within their own community.

The category of brother-only institutes represents a wide range in terms of membership size. For example, the Brothers of the Christians Schools had 2,212 members in 1970, while the smallest recurring group, the Brothers of the Congregation of Our Lady of the Holy Rosary, had 13 members in 1970. Although these two institutes represent opposite end-points in the data, they are both part of an intriguing case study when it comes to brother-only religious institutes.

In 1970, the total membership in the twenty brother-only institutes included in the OCD was 6,248. By 2015, nineteen brother-only institutes were listed in the OCD, and their overall membership had decreased by 70 percent to 1,896 brothers. As noted previously, the overall rate of decline among religious institutes of men across this time period was 55 percent, so the brother-only institutes decreased 15 percentage points more than the overall average. The combined membership among the nineteen brother-only institutes in 2015 (1,896 members) was less than the number reported by just one brother-only institute in 1970—the Brothers of the Christian Schools reported 2,212 members in that year.

Monastic Institutes

The final category of religious institutes of men explored here is the monastic institutes. In the United States, these institutes include the Benedictine Monks, the Cistercian Order of the Strict Observance, the Cistercian Fathers, the Camaldolese Hermits of the Congregation of Montecorona, and the Order of Carthusians. For this study, the monastics are grouped here into five institutes, but in reality each of these comprises a number of distinct abbeys. For example, the Benedictine Monks are located in fifty-five different abbeys across this forty-five-year period. These abbeys average about thirty-five men religious per abbey over the period of this study.

A small but consistent trend noted in this examination of the data is that membership in these monastic institutes constitutes an increasing proportion of the total population of men in religious institutes, as can be seen in Figure 2.12. Over

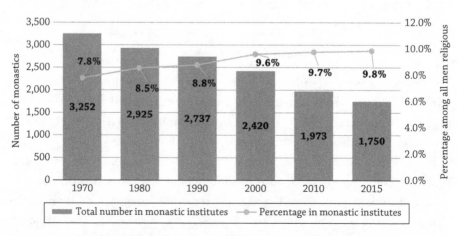

FIGURE 2.12. Number in Monastic Institutes and Percentage of All Men Religious
Source: The Official Catholic Directory (relevant years).

the past forty-five years, the proportion of all men religious who are members of monastic institutes increased from 7.8 percent to 9.8 percent of all men religious.

The number of men in religious institutes in the United States has declined sharply over the past forty-five years, but not all institutes experienced this decline equally. Some had a gradual decline in membership and a few others even experienced growth in membership. Several religious institutes of men went out of existence in the United States during this time, and a few new institutes were created.

CHARACTERISTICS OF MEN AND WOMEN RELIGIOUS

A 2009 study that CARA completed for the National Religious Vocation Conference (NRVC) reported that there are now more Catholic sisters in the United States over age ninety than under age sixty (see Figure 2.13). Half of all religious institutes of women that responded to that survey reported a median age of seventy-three (Bendyna and Gautier 2009). In essence, this means that approximately half of the women religious in the United States in 2009 were age seventy-three or older.

The situation is not quite as extreme among men religious, although the same study finds that three in four men religious are age sixty or older (see Figure 2.14). Half of all religious institutes of men who responded to the survey reported a median age of sixty-six among their members.

While many religious institutes continue to produce new members, these new vocations tend to be around thirty years old when they enter religious life, quite a bit older than the average age of entrance in the 1950s when it was more common to enter religious life right out of high school (Gautier and Do 2016). Overall, more

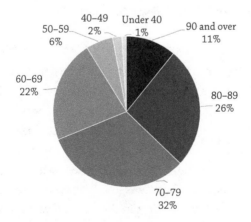

FIGURE 2.13. Age Distribution of Women Religious, 2009
Source: Bendyna and Gautier (2009).

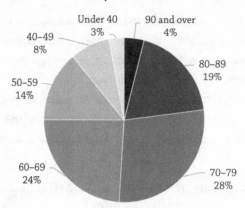

FIGURE 2.14. Age Distribution of Men Religious, 2009
Source: Bendyna and Gautier (2009).

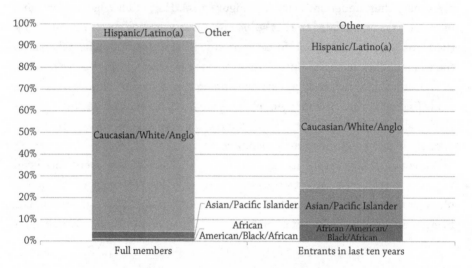

FIGURE 2.15. Race/Ethnicity of Full Members Compared to Entrants in the Last Ten Years
Source: Gautier, Wiggins, and Holland (2014).

than two in three religious institutes have no one who entered the institute in 2015. Just a handful of institutes of have more than three who entered during that year.

Another factor that is perhaps moderating the rate of decline among religious in recent years is an increase in international vocations. A research study that CARA completed for NRVC in 2014 found that while nine in ten full members of religious institutes are Caucasian/Anglo, four in ten of those who entered in the last ten years are of another race or ethnicity (see Figure 2.15). More than half of these institutes say that at least one entrant in the past ten years was born outside the United States (Gautier, Wiggins, and Holland 2014). Many U.S.-based institutes include members from outside the United States in their member counts. In many cases, the numbers provided to the OCD by religious institutes include the members of the institute who are serving abroad. While these numbers add to the overall size of the religious institute, they further complicate the effort to understand what is happening in terms of growth and decline in religious institutes in the United States.

CONCLUSIONS

Population trends indicate clearly that religious institutes in the United States are undergoing a transformation. The overall trend is one of decline from a high point in the late 1960s, but this line masks important differences among the institutes themselves. Some have experienced a steep decline in numbers or even gone out of existence, while others have remained relatively stable and a few are even growing. Likewise, the overall trend of an aging, mostly white, population masks the reality that increasing numbers of men and women of diverse ethnicities continue to be attracted to religious life, gradually transforming the institutes from within. The next chapter examines the family background and experience of these newer members, in order to learn more about some of their life experiences that influenced their choice of a vocation.

3

The Influences of Families on Religious Vocations

Patricia Wittberg

IT HAS LONG been recognized that the roots of a vocation to the priesthood or religious life can often be traced to the attitudes about God and religion that the novice or seminarian absorbed very early in life. The primary source of these attitudes, of course, is the family. Around the world and across the centuries, societies in which families considered Church service a high and holy calling and encouraged their children to enter it produced numerous vocations. Societies in which families were suspicious of priests and religious or valued more lucrative and prestigious careers for their offspring produced fewer vocations.[1] More recently, Pope Saint John Paul II's 1999 apostolic exhortation *Ecclesia in America* "notes the central vocational role of families. A Christian family that celebrates the Eucharist, embraces the sacraments, prays together, and practices God's love while caring for others is without doubt a privileged context where the young 'discover a vocation of service in the community and the Church'" (Ospino 2015:13).

To what extent does this continue to be true in the United States today? CARA has conducted several studies that help chart the influence of families on religious vocations. The largest study was conducted in 2015 for the National Religious Vocation Conference (NRVC) and surveyed the members of men's and women's religious orders, diocesan priests, and seminarians who had entered their novitiate

---

[1] For examples of societies where priests and religious were held in suspicion, see Orsi (1985), Brettell (1990:64), and Behar (1990:91–96).

or seminary after 2000. These priests, seminarians, and religious were then asked to provide the contact information for a member of their families (usually one of their parents), and these relatives were also surveyed. Following the survey, two focus groups of family members were also conducted, one in Washington, DC, and one in Chicago. The survey responses of the new priests and religious were compared to previous national surveys of all Catholics that CARA had conducted, to see whether and how the family backgrounds of priests and religious differed from those of other Catholic families. One such national survey had been conducted for Holy Cross Family Ministries (HCFM) to serve as a resource for the World Meeting of Families (Philadelphia, September 2015) and also for the Synod of Bishops on the Family held at the Vatican (October 2015). This study surveyed a sample of U.S. Catholic adults who were parents of a minor child. Other surveys included a nationwide survey of all U.S. Catholics (D'Antonio, Dillon, and Gautier 2013), a study of never-married Catholics (Gray and Gautier 2012), and several studies[2] of newly ordained or professed U.S. religious.

FINDINGS

In general, respondents to the NRVC survey were more likely than the average U.S. Catholic adult to be white, non-Hispanic (see Table 3.1). They also tended to be better educated than the average adult Catholic. Most (81 percent of the priests and seminarians and 79 percent of the male and female religious) were born in the United States, and most (about four out of five) spoke English in their homes growing up.[3] However, the seminarians surveyed were almost twice as likely as the diocesan priests to report being Hispanic/Latino (15 percent as compared to 8 percent). While almost all (97 percent) of the non-Hispanic Caucasian male and female religious were born in the United States, only 43 percent of the Hispanic/Latino religious and 37 percent of the Asian/Pacific Islander religious were U.S.-born. Of the diocesan priests and seminarians in the survey, 95 percent of the white, non-Hispanic respondents were born in the United States, compared to 37 percent of the Hispanics/Latinos and 22 percent of the Asian/Pacific Islanders who were born here. Half of those not born here had moved to the United States after the year 2000.

In general, both the priests/seminarians and the members of religious orders reported having one or two siblings. Only 4 or 5 percent were the only child in

---

[2] Among them, Bendyna and Gautier (2009), Gautier and Cidade (2010), and Gautier and Saunders (2013).
[3] Of the 20 percent who were non-English speakers, between 7 and 9 percent spoke Spanish at home growing up. The remainder (between 10 and 12 percent) spoke (in descending order of frequency) Vietnamese, Igbo, Mandarin Chinese, Korean, and Malayam.

TABLE 3.1

Demographic Characteristics of Participants in the NRVC Study, Compared to U.S. Catholics

	Men/Women Religious %	Priests/ Seminarians %	Family Members %	U.S. Catholics %
Race/Ethnicity				
White, non-Hispanic	77	79	88	62*
Hispanic/Latino	9	11	6	32*
Other				6*
Asian	11	6	3	
African-American	4	2	1	
Native American	<1	<1	<1	
Nativity and Language Spoken at Home				
U.S.-born	79	81	n.a.	72+
English	82	81	92	n.a.
Spanish	7	9	3	n.a.
Other language	12	10	4	n.a.
Level of Education				
High school or less	13	25	9	46*
Trade/technical degree	1	2	5	7*
Some college	17	18	18	19*
Bachelor's degree	49	38	37	18*
Graduate degree	20	17	31	10*
Family Size				
Only child	4	5	n.a.	6**
>8 siblings	4	5		
Family Structure				
Two-parent family	89	90	n.a.	n.a.
Single-parent family	6	7		
Other	5	–		

Sources: * D'Antonio, Dillon, and Gautier (2013:177); ** Gray and Gautier (2012:25); + data from the 2012 General Social Survey; all other data from Gautier, Wiggins, and Holland (2014).

their family. This is roughly comparable to the percentage of all Catholic adults nationally who report being only children. Another 4 or 5 percent of the priests, seminarians, and religious order members reported having more than eight siblings. Almost all (89–90 percent) came from two-parent families.

The respondents' families tended to do more things together than most Catholic families do: Three-fourths of the respondents to the NRVC family survey reported that they ate dinner together daily when their children were growing up, as compared to barely half (51 percent) of the Catholic parents in the HCFM nationwide study. Almost two-thirds of the NRVC family members (63 percent) also reported engaging as a family in other activities at least once a week; this was similar to the percentage of all Catholic parents (62 percent) who reported such structured family time.

Two in three of the religious order respondents in the NRVC study were women; one-third were men. As would be expected, all of the priest/seminarian respondents were male. Of the family members surveyed in the NRVC study, 55 percent were the mothers or stepmothers of the priest or religious, 20 percent were the fathers or stepfathers, and nearly all the rest were siblings. The median age of the religious order respondents was 33 for the women and 34 for the men. The median age for the priests/seminarians was 32, and for the family members it was 57.

In addition to age, CARA typically categorizes Catholic survey respondents into four generations, based on life experiences that are particularly relevant to Catholics:

- The Pre-Vatican II generation includes those born before 1943. Its members were over the age of 72 in 2015 when the survey was conducted. They came of age prior to the Second Vatican Council, and had been raised in a Church that changed dramatically in their later adulthood. Members of this generation played a crucial role in creating and sustaining many of the institutions of twentieth-century Catholic life. Just one percent of the respondents to either the priest/seminarian survey or the survey of members of religious orders were members of the Pre-Vatican II generation (see Table 3.2). They had entered the priesthood or religious life after 2000, when they were at least 58 years old.

- Members of the Vatican II generation were born between 1943 and 1960 and were between the ages of 55 and 72 in 2015. Members of this generation came of age during the time of the Second Vatican Council and their formative years spanned a period of profound changes in the Church (as well as in the larger society and culture). To a large extent, this generation overlaps with the category "Baby Boomers" that is used in secular studies of U.S. generations. Almost one-tenth of the men and women religious (6 percent of the men and 11 percent of the women), and 7 percent of the priests/seminarians, in the survey are of the Vatican II generation. This means that they entered the priesthood or religious life when they were in their 40s, 50s, and 60s.

- The Post-Vatican II generation, born between 1961 and 1981, consists of those who were ages 34 to 54 in 2015. Members of this generation, sometimes called

TABLE 3.2

Generation of Participants in the NRVC Study, Compared to U.S. Catholics

	Women Religious %	Men Religious %	Priests %	Seminarians %	U.S. Catholics* %
Pre-Vatican II	1	< 1	< 1	< 1	10
Vatican II	11	6	2	2	33
Post-Vatican II	36	47	12	12	34
Millennial	52	47	85	85	23

Sources: * Data in this column from D'Antonio, Dillon, and Gautier (2013:177); all other data from Gautier, Wiggins, and Holland (2014).

"Generation X" in the secular literature, have almost no lived experience of the pre-Vatican II Church. Their religious training occurred primarily during the 1970s and 1980s, a time when religious education patterns and methods were very different from those used prior in earlier decades. Four in ten of the men and women religious (47 percent of the men and 36 percent of the women), 56 percent of the priests, and 12 percent of the seminarians in the survey are of the Post-Vatican II generation.

• The Millennial generation, those born after 1981, is the youngest generation of adult Catholics. This generation came of age under the papacies of John Paul II and Benedict XVI. Most are less steeped in the Catholic culture of earlier generations of Catholics and are less knowledgeable about their faith. Millennials make up half of the men and women religious surveyed (47 percent of the men and 52 percent of the women), as well as 33 percent of the priests and 85 percent of the seminarians.

Family Religious Background

There is no such thing as a "typical" family of a priest or a religious, nor is there a specific recipe parents can follow to assure that one of their offspring will receive a call to the priesthood or religious life. There are some overall patterns, however. About the same percentage of the new priests, seminarians, and religious surveyed had come from families where both parents were Catholics as was the case for U.S. Catholic adults in general. But the religious, priests, and seminarians were three times as likely as U.S. Catholic adults in general to report having another priest or religious in their extended family, and the family members surveyed were twice as likely to do so. Respondents from Asian backgrounds were exceptionally likely to say that another family member was a priest or religious: About half reported having at least one such relative. In addition to having relatives who were priests or religious, six in ten of the responding family members in the NRVC survey noted that they had invited sisters, brothers, or priests from the local parish or school for a meal or other social event. Several focus group participants also mentioned that frequent contact with priests or religious was normal in their families:

> The fact that in my family were priests and sisters, it seems that it was easier for [family member] to make the decision. Among other friends, the decision to become a sister is very strange, but for her it was not. I remember a long time ago seeing that the brother of my grandfather was a priest. All my life I've been seeing fathers and sisters, so it's normal. The fact that they were there was something that I think made it easier for her to make the decision.

> We often had priests to dinner. It wasn't like they were separated that much from us. They were friends. So our kids got used to having priests at dinner.

The survey respondents, both the families and the religious or priests/seminarians, were also more likely than the average Catholic to report having attended Catholic grade schools, high schools, and colleges (Table 3.3). This was especially true of the men who had entered religious orders. The diocesan priests and seminarians were somewhat more likely than the average Catholic to report having attended parish religious education classes as children. A comparatively higher percentage of seminarians, and of women who had entered religious orders since 2000, reported

TABLE 3.3

Catholic School Experience of Participants in the NRVC Study, Compared to U.S. Catholics

	Women	Men			U.S.
	Religious	Religious	Priests	Seminarians	Catholics
	%	%	%	%	%
Attended Catholic schools					
Elementary/middle school	54	51	49	43	37[*]
High school	39	48	38	35	19[*]
College/university	45	58	47	38	8[*]
Parish religious education	59	59	67	66	58[**]
Home schooled	13	6	5	14	n.a.

Sources: [*] D'Antonio, Dillon, and Gautier (2013:177); [**] Gray and Gautier (2012:25); all other data from Gautier, Wiggins, and Holland (2014).

being home-schooled. These tended to be men and women of the Millennial generation, rather than the older respondents.

Many of the religious order members and the diocesan priests/seminarians reported having had some sort of family trauma growing up: Between 16 and 21 percent reported having a sibling who died, while one in eight reported the death or serious illness of a parent. One in eight had also experienced the divorce of their parents.

Family Religious Practices

In comparison to the average adult Catholic in the United States, the families of the new priests, seminarians, and religious order members were much more likely to have attended Mass at least weekly when their children were growing up: Between 84 and 96 percent reported attending Mass together as a family weekly or more often. The Hispanic/Latino(a) religious were less likely to report high levels of Mass attendance as a family (66 percent) than the European or Asian/Pacific Islander respondents were (87 percent). The priest/seminarian respondents showed a similar pattern: 92 percent of Asian respondents and 88 percent of European-American respondents reported attending Mass as a family weekly or more than weekly, as compared to 73 percent of the Hispanic/Latino respondents. Still, all of these percentages are higher than the average Mass attendance reported by all Catholic adults: Only one-third or fewer in in the national surveys of Catholic adults reported attending Mass at least weekly.

While it is relatively common for Catholic families to say "grace" together before eating a family meal, many of the families of the religious order members, priests, and seminarians also prayed together as a family at other times while they were growing up (Table 3.4). Almost half did so at least a few times per month. In general, Asian respondents were more likely than other cultural groups to report higher levels of family prayer. While only a fifth or fewer European-American and Hispanic/Latino(a) religious order respondents reported praying together daily as a family (20 percent and 16 percent, respectively), Asian religious order respondents reported a frequency that was at least twice as high. At the other extreme, nearly half (48 percent) of the European-American religious order respondents and almost four in ten (37 percent) of the Hispanic/Latino(a) religious order respondents reported that their families seldom or never prayed at home together, while only a quarter of Asian respondents said this. Similar ethnic discrepancies occurred among the priest/seminarian respondents.

The family members in the NRVC survey also reported a much higher frequency of private, personal prayer than did the respondents to the HCFM or other

TABLE 3.4

Family Religious Practices of Participants in the NRVC Study, by Race/Ethnicity

	Men/Women Religious %	Priests/ Seminarians %	Family Members %
Grace before/after meals			
White, non-Hispanic	74	74	87
Hispanic/Latino	20	38	67*
Asian/Pacific Islander	60	65	
Display religious art in the home			
White, non-Hispanic	57	55	78
Hispanic/Latino	68	50	69
Asian/Pacific Islander	69	66	
Active participation in parish life			
White, non-Hispanic	49	53	73
Hispanic/Latino	25	32	51
Asian/Pacific Islander	42	52	
Sacramentals			
White, non-Hispanic	47	48	69
Hispanic/Latino	50	48	58
Asian/Pacific Islander	53	63	
Processions			
White, non-Hispanic	19	19	32
Hispanic/Latino	49	54	47
Asian/Pacific Islander	41	55	
Marian devotions			
White, non-Hispanic	15	11	21
Hispanic/Latino	55	52	36
Asian/Pacific Islander	52	58	
Catholic advocacy			
White, non-Hispanic	12	6	17
Hispanic/Latino	5	4	9
Asian/Pacific Islander	4	12	
Home altars			
White, non-Hispanic	9	4	12
Hispanic/Latino	37	30	38
Asian/Pacific Islander	57	57	

Source: * Only white/non-white categories of race/ethnicity for family members in this study; data from Gautier, Wiggins, and Holland (2014).

national surveys. The priests, seminarians, and religious order members were not asked this question, but it is presumed that they pray daily.

Several patterns occurred in all three surveys between the *kinds* of family prayers and religious practices reported by respondents of different ethnic groups (Table 3.4). The non-Hispanic white priests, seminarians, religious order members, and their families were the most likely to report that their families had said grace before and after meals and participated actively in parish life. They were the *least* likely to pray the rosary or novenas together as a family, to have home altars, or to engage in processions and Marian devotions. The Hispanic and Asian/Pacific Islander priests, seminarians, religious order members, and their families were equally highly likely to report engaging in processions and Marian devotions, but they were both less likely than white, Non-Hispanic respondents to report being active in parish life. Asian/Pacific Islander respondents were the most likely of all three ethnic categories to report having had religious art in the home while growing up, to have made use of sacramentals, to have prayed the rosary or novenas together as a family, or to have had home altars. Hispanic families were the least likely to say grace before and after meals or to participate actively in parish life. While white, non-Hispanic religious order members were the most likely to report that their families had engaged in Catholic advocacy while they were growing up, it was the Asian/Pacific Islander priests and seminarians who reported this for their families. The percentage of either ethnic group engaging in Catholic advocacy, however, was very small (12 percent).

Close to three-fourths of the religious order members, priests, and seminarians reported that religion was "somewhat" or "very" important to their fathers, and nine in ten reported it was "somewhat" or "very" important to their mothers (Table 3.5). Among the family members who responded to the NRVC survey, 92 percent said that religious faith was either "the most important" or "among the most important" aspects of their lives. In contrast, only 49 percent of the respondents in the HCFM parents' survey, and only 41 percent of all adult Catholics surveyed nationally, said that the Catholic Church was that important to them. The family members of the priests, seminarians, and religious surveyed in the NRVC survey were twice as likely as all adult Catholics to say that it was very important that the younger generations of their family grow up Catholic.

In summary, the family life that today's new priests, seminarians, and men and women religious experienced in their childhoods differed from the family life of most American Catholics in several key ways:

- The families were three times more likely than the average Catholic family to attend Mass weekly or more often.

TABLE 3.5

Importance of Religion in the Family in the NRVC Study, Compared to U.S. Catholics

	Priests/ Seminarians	Family Members	HFCM Parents	U.S. Catholics*
	%	%	%	%
Religion important to father				
Not at all/only a little	23			
Somewhat important	27			
Very important	51			
Religion important to mother				
Not at all/only a little	11			
Somewhat important	23			
Very important	69			
How important is religious faith/the Catholic Church to you?				
Not at all/only a little		2	11	19
Somewhat important		7	39	40
Among the most/the most important		92	49	41
How important is it that the younger generations of your family grow up Catholic?				
Not at all/only a little		4		23
Somewhat important		9		37
Very important		87		40

Sources: * Data in this column from D'Antonio, Dillon, and Gautier (2013;171); all other data from Gautier, Wiggins, and Holland (2014).

- The family members were more than twice as likely to say they pray daily or more often.
- The families were also at least three times more likely to have included another priest or religious while the current respondents were growing up.
- The family members of the priests, seminarians, and religious order members were twice as likely to say that it was very important to pass on the Catholic faith to future generations.

- The family members of the priests, seminarians, and religious order members were more than twice as likely as the average Catholic adult to say that religious faith was the most important or among the most important things in their lives.

While overall the priests, seminarians, and religious order members were more likely to have experienced various religious and devotional practices when they were growing up, the various ethnic groups among the NRVC respondents differed in the kinds of these practices. The families of Hispanic priests, seminarians, and religious were less likely to have participated in parish life or to have engaged in Catholic advocacy activities; Asian/Pacific Islander priests, seminarians, and religious were more likely to have had home altars, religious art, and sacramentals, or to have participated in family rosaries or novenas. Both Asian and Hispanic respondents were more likely to have engaged in processions and Marian devotions than their white, non-Hispanic counterparts were. But, whatever ethnic version of Catholic devotion and practice was available to them while they were growing up, the priests, seminarians, and religious order respondents were more likely than U.S. Catholic adults on average to report that their families had engaged in the practice of their faith.

Influences on Vocations

But did these familial religious practices influence the decision of the family member to enter the priesthood or religious life? Might other familial practices, such as the active encouraging or discouraging of their members to consider (or reject) a religious vocation, have a greater impact? The NRVC surveys asked the religious order members and the priests/seminarians what in their family background had been the most influential in their discernment of a vocation. The surveys also asked whether the respondents' parents or other family members had ever spoken to them about priesthood or religious life, and whether and how family members had supported or discouraged them in their vocational discernment.

Influential Background Factors

In the NRVC survey, the priests, seminarians, and religious order members were asked what practices in their family background had been the most influential in their vocational discernment. For all respondents, the most common response was the faith of their parents: almost half of the priests and seminarians and a quarter of the religious order members listed this as the most important influence. Family love and support was also highly mentioned, as was the respondent's own regular Mass attendance and devotion to Mary. Lesser numbers cited attendance at Catholic school and positive relationships with priests and religious. Priests and seminarians also cited family values and volunteering; religious order members cited the faith of other relatives and attending a Catholic school.

> I think that it was my parents' desire to follow God and be faithful to Him. I was taught by my mom that God loved me and always wanted what was best for me. I think having this spiritual foundation was essential to having an open heart to seek God's will when He started guiding me towards religious life.

> The most influential thing in my discernment from my family background would have to be the faithfulness of my family to Sunday Mass, no matter where we were, as well as the faithfulness to many other aspects of the faith.

> Faithful Mass attendance. We never missed. If my father worked, he got up for 7:30 Mass. If we were on vacation, we found a church.

> The most influential thing in my family was the openness and the support. My family was with me 100 percent.

> I knew that my parents loved me and supported me in whatever I chose to do. They did not try to force me to be anything but supported me when I made a decision.

Family Discussion and Encouragement of Vocations

The family members of religious, priests, and seminarians were asked if they had ever discussed religious vocations as a family, if they had ever encouraged a family member to consider religious life or the priesthood, and how supportive, in general, the family was to the idea or priesthood or religious life as a vocation (Table 3.6). Over half of the family members surveyed reported engaging in vocational discussions. This was almost twice as large a percentage as in a survey of all Catholic adults (33 percent).[4] Interestingly, a much smaller proportion of the responding religious than the diocesan priests and seminarians reported that their families had discussed vocations with them.

---

[4] And even the one-third figure for all Catholic adults is probably inflated, since this survey asked about encouraging vocations to the diaconate in addition to vocations to the priesthood and religious life (Gray and Perl 2008).

TABLE 3.6

Family Encouragement/Discouragement of Vocations

	Men/Women Religious %	Priests/ Seminarians %	Family Members %
Have you ever encouraged a family member to consider religious life or priesthood?			56
In general, how supportive was the family to the idea of priesthood or religious life as a vocation?			
Very			66
Somewhat			24
A little			8
Not at all			2
Family ever had discussions about vocations to religious life/priesthood?			54
Family members who ever spoke about vocations to religious life/priesthood			
Respondent's mother	30	41	
Respondent's father	20	29	
Another family member	29	62	
Overall, starting a discussion about your vocation was easy for you	41	56	

Source: Data from Gautier, Wiggins, and Holland (2014).

Both the religious order members and the priests/seminarians stated that starting a discussion with their family about their religious vocation had been difficult for them. Still, the conversation was easier when a parent had at least broached the subject beforehand. Among the respondents who said their mother had *ever* spoken to them about a vocation, over 60 percent (63 percent for the religious order members, and 68 percent for the priests and seminarians) said that starting a family discussion about vocation was easy for them, as compared to 41 percent for the overall sample of religious order members and 56 percent of the priests and seminarians. The percentages for those whose father had ever spoken to them about a vocation were similar (67 and 71 percent, as compared to 41 and 56 percent).

Family Members' Encouragement or Discouragement

In the past ten years, CARA has conducted numerous surveys on the subject of vocations. In addition to those that have been mentioned so far, several other surveys of priests and religious have included a question on whether or not the respondents' family members had ever encouraged or discouraged their vocational discernment. An additional survey, conducted in 2012 of never-married Catholic men and women who had *not* entered religious life or priesthood, also included a question about amount of family vocational encouragement. While the various surveys differed slightly in which particular family members they asked about, several overall patterns emerge:

- Family members of priests and religious were almost twice as likely as the average Catholic to say they had encouraged a family member to consider a religious vocation. In other words, never-married Catholics who had *not* entered religious life or the priesthood reported vocational encouragement by parents and other relatives that was several times lower than in the surveys of priests and religious. Family encouragement *does* matter to young Catholics in their vocational discernment.
- Mothers/stepmothers are more likely than other family members to encourage vocations.
- Family members are *less* likely to have encouraged vocations to religious life than to the priesthood. They are also more likely to have *discouraged* vocations to religious life than to the priesthood. Mothers, especially, are more than three times more likely to have discouraged vocations to religious life than to the priesthood.

Another pattern was that non-Hispanic white respondents to the family survey were more likely than non-white respondents to indicate that the father/step-father of the person considering a vocation had encouraged this discernment. Likewise, non-white family members were more likely than white family members to say that the father/stepfather had *dis*couraged the vocation.

While the priests, seminarians, men and women religious, and their families in the NRVC survey all admitted that at least some family member had been less than supportive in the respondent's initial discernment, all agreed that the families were now strongly supportive, averaging over 90-percent support from parents and siblings. Other relatives remained slightly less likely to be supportive, but the priests, seminarians and women and men religious reported

TABLE 3.7

Types of Family Encouragement/Discouragement of Vocations (Percentage mentioning each item)

	Men/Women Religious %	Priests/ Seminarians %
Briefly describe how your family *supported* your vocational discernment:		
Verbal encouragement	27	35
Prayer	21	28
Openness/acceptance	15	11
Vocation visits	14	7
Allowing space/freedom	13	9
Listening/discussing	13	11
Financial support	11	12
Briefly describe how your family *discouraged* your vocational discernment:		
Said it was a waste of time/talent	20	7
Encouraged marriage/career	14	25
Verbal criticism	14	25
Feared respondent was rushed into a vocation	10	
Listed other, better options		11

Source: Data from Gautier, Wiggins, and Holland (2014).

between two-thirds and three-fourths of their more distant relatives now supported their vocational choice.

Types of Family Encouragement and Discouragement

The NRVC survey asked the priests, seminarians, and religious order members to describe *how* their families had encouraged and/or discouraged their vocational discernment (Table 3.7).

The most common types of encouragement reported were verbal encouragement and prayer, which were cited by 27 and 21 percent, respectively, of the religious order members, and by 35 and 28 percent of the priests and seminarians:

By praying for me and loving me. I knew that whatever I discerned was God's will for me and they would still love me.

Family members (particularly my grandmother) supported me through prayer.

By letting me know that they loved me and were supportive of whatever I follow God in.

Other common answers included simply being open to the idea (cited by 15 percent of the religious order members and 11 percent of the priests/seminarians), listening to and discussing with the respondent about his/her discernment (cited by 13 and 11 percent), and allowing him/her the space and freedom to decide (cited by 13 and 9 percent):

All they wanted for me was to find what gave me joy. They supported me in all my relationships until I found my true self in this religious life.

My family allowed me to explore my vocation without any pressure in one direction or another.

My brother and his wife were my biggest support. They listened to me quite a bit during my discernment process and gave me objective feedback to help me realize that God was indeed calling me to religious life.

I announced to them that I was going to start the process and they were extremely open and helpful about it. They gave me information to aid me and tried being near me along the process.

Approximately one in ten respondents mentioned that their parents had also given them financial support:

Financial support enabling me to enter seminary when it became clear it was not an idle phase but a serious endeavor.

They made it possible. Helped with expenses. Overall, they have been present.

Help with paying my student loans so I could enter the convent.

The most commonly mentioned type of *discouragement* mentioned by priests and seminarians was the parents' wish that their son would choose marriage and a career instead of the celibate priesthood, followed by verbal criticism of the priesthood as a lifestyle. These two types of discouragement were less commonly mentioned by the religious order members surveyed:

Comments about whether I would be happier being married and the fact that I would not have children to carry on the family name.

Brother and cousins focused on celibacy. They cannot imagine why I'd want that! For those with faith it is a great gift. For the worldly person it seems crazy.

From their experience, they had plenty to say about less-than-holy priests and religious and "why give up so much?" Comments were sometimes harsh, even hurtful.

Making comments about the priestly life being a life of ease.

It was clear that my family wanted me to continue my legal career rather than become a priest.

My father thought it was absolutely nuts for me to abandon my work on a Ph.D. in history.

For the religious order members, in contrast, the most commonly mentioned type of discouragement was that such a lifestyle would be a waste of the member's time and talent:

My family basically believed that I was going to be oppressed if I entered the convent and that I could do so many other more valuable things with my life.

They told me that there were many more options for women now and that religious life is oppressive.

They are very concerned that I will not have a nice job, a wife and children, and prominent social status. It was kind of shame when they knew I gave up my previous career to join a religious order.

About one in ten religious order members said their family worried they were being "rushed into" a decision.

Misconceptions about Religious Life and Priesthood

Some family members discourage vocations due to misconceptions they have about religious life and priesthood. The NRVC survey of the family members included a question asking about these misconceptions. Although four in ten family members said they had had no misconceptions, others cited mistaken ideas of how religious life would affect their relative's relationship with the rest of the family. On the one hand, some thought that ministerial assignments far from home and the all-encompassing nature of a priestly or religious vocation would distance their son, daughter, or sibling from the rest of the family—and later found they had been mistaken. Others, however, had expected that their son, daughter, or sibling would still be able to attend all family gatherings and were surprised when s/he could not do so:

Everyone believed that our daughter would still be as much a part of our family life as she had been previously—visiting at Christmas, Easter, birthdays, baptisms, confirmations, weddings. It wasn't until she entered the convent that we all realized her Order is now her family; we only get to see her at specified times that are set aside as visiting days (these don't include any of the above-mentioned times).

For me, and probably our parents, one misconception that [Name] has proven wrong since entering the novitiate was the notion that we wouldn't see him very much. Or, when we would see him, he would act differently or be so "priestly" or pious that we wouldn't be able to connect with him on certain issues of the day, or he'd no longer enjoy silly comedies, or act "silly," or enjoy a night on the town. He's proven this notion wrong.

He entered a religious community and we all thought we would remain very close. We are disappointed that his formation seemed to distance him from our family. Due to his commitment to the community and his vows of obedience he has little freedom to be with his family. We had no idea prior to his entering the order that he would have such little freedom to do/have what he wants and make his own decisions and choices.

He could still be an active member of our family. Even though his vocation to the priesthood was paramount, he could still have friends and be involved with our family.

At least one in seven family members cited other misconceptions about how involved and present their son, daughter, or sibling would continue to be to the rest of the family.

Incorrect impressions of seminary and religious community life, or beliefs that priests and religious were not "normal" people, were also cited by one in ten respondents to the family members' survey:

I learned that sisters are regular people and like to laugh and have fun. I realize the amount of sacrifice women make when they choose to enter a convent—like a vow of poverty, giving up personal possessions, limited contact with family and friends, etc.

I realized an emphasis on masculinity (not all feminine men as I perceived). I saw they were ordinary, fun men (not super-holy odd ducks that I had thought).

Worries about the Future of Priesthood and Religious Life

Family members also listed several worries about the future. While three in ten families said they had no such worries, others admitted that they had. The two most commonly cited worries were the amount of overwork/stress experienced by priests and religious, and a fear of persecution by the larger secular culture, which some family members perceived as being hostile to religion.

> *Due to the shortage of priests/religious, there is a high demand in parishes. I do worry that the work will be too much for one person to handle.*

> *I am concerned that there will not be enough sisters to maintain their order.*

> *I don't want him to experience burnout and/or loneliness. Priests have so many stresses in their lives. Our culture is very challenging and he must be very strong spiritually, mentally, and physically.*

> *As the divergence between the Church and society widens, I'm concerned that the religious might be among the first to face persecution.*

> *I think my son will make a wonderful priest, but I pray to our Blessed Mother that she will protect him from any false accusation. There are untrustworthy people out there who want to hurt our Catholic faith.*

Other commonly cited worries were that their son, daughter, or sibling would be lonely, would miss the family, or would suffer from a lack of encouragement or support:

> *I worry about what happens when he's old and he has no immediate family to take care of him. I worry about him being lonely and alone.*

> *My hope is that he continues to be happy, meaning a good assignment, a supportive pastor, etc. Since entering the seminary, he's been the happiest I've known him to be. So I hope that continues.*

> *Her missing her family so much. We are a very close family and do many things to-gether as a family. If I'm not here, will other family members pay attention to her the way I do? Who will take care of her if she would have a serious illness?*

> *Aloneness. As he ages and we age, what about family support for medical needs and other needs? He has one sister who lives 900 miles away. How will they support each other?*

> *Because she is in a small, aging order, I fear for the future of her order.*

Our son has a spiritual life that is rare in today's world. He will be a great priest when ordained. Dos the Archdiocese provide mentoring programs for new priests? The point is that it's difficult to find and develop good priests, so let's be sure to invest in mentoring and maintaining spiritual growth.

Slightly less than one in ten also worried that their relative would not persevere in his/her vocation:

How they will be able to practice/live out their Roman Catholic faith in the face of the increasingly confused state of the Church in the post-Vatican II era.

I don't worry about them, but I pray that they will always be faithful to their vocation.

I worry that there may be other "distractions" that might pull her in a different direction.

My only concern is that he can continue in his vocation for life. A vocation is a life-long commitment and it doesn't come easily all the time. My hope and prayer is that he finds contentment in his vocation.

RECOMMENDATIONS BY FAMILY MEMBERS
TO ENCOURAGE VOCATIONS

The final question in the family members' survey asked respondents to suggest ways that family members could support or promote vocations to the priesthood and religious life. The surveys of women and men religious, diocesan priests, and seminarians asked how their families could have been more helpful in their vocational discernment. Together, the answers to these questions provide recommendations for families on how to encourage religious vocations.

Prayer

One of the most common recommendations, mentioned by half the family respondents and a fourth of the religious order members, priests, and seminarians was prayer—both together as a family while one's children are growing up, and also individual prayer for priests and religious and for family members still discerning a vocation:

Families should pray together, have dinner together and go to Mass together. With all the electronic gadgets that "bring people together," it seems that families are growing farther apart.

I think an increase in prayer together as a family, or witnessing my parents' prayer would have been helpful.

A more serious commitment to family prayer would have been helpful, e.g., praying the rosary more often (we did sometimes) or reading the Bible together.

Encouragement/Listening

A second common recommendation (mentioned by a third of the family members, a fifth of the religious order members, and an eighth of the priests/seminarians) was encouragement and listening:

Allowing people to explore different paths, being supportive and not putting labels on things. I see that people think that religious people or priests are somewhat different but they are not[;] they are just following a different path focusing on less mundane things. We should embrace and support that with the same enthusiasm we support college students, tradesmen, singles, mothers, etc.

Even though I began thinking about a religious vocation when I was eleven or twelve, I didn't say anything about it for years, for fear of negative reactions from my family, especially my siblings. More support in my home would have resolved much of my hesitancy early on in my discernment.

I would have liked to feel my family's support in a more tangible way other than saying they are praying for me and/or support my decision to enter seminary.

Be open to it, but I don't think you can really PUSH it. The main thing is to encourage our children to do what is right for them to do—that's where our true happiness and fulfillment are. Also, of course, pray for them and encourage them to pray about it also.

By loving, listening, and encouraging them not to be afraid to be who God created them to be. Let the Lord have the room to work in their hearts. It is a temptation as parents to decide who or what your child will "be" when he or she grows up. It is best to leave that up to the Lord.

Communication/Education about the Faith and Vocations

One-fourth of both the priests/seminarians and the religious order members said that more education in the faith would be helpful. One in seven thought that more talk about religious vocations would have helped them in their discernment. Similar percentages of the family members agreed that talking about religious life and communication/education about the faith were important:

A deeper understanding of the traditions of the Church. I did not experience my first holy hour until I entered seminary, the sacrament of penance growing up was scarce, etc. If these foundational elements had been part of family life, I feel like my discernment would have been easier.

Actively asking me if I thought I had a calling to be a priest; making it understood that it was an option and that it was normal.

An attempt to understand the larger Church and not just the minimal components of a faith life that comes from once-a-week Mass.

Creating a culture of vocations as a family during my childhood. I never heard my parents talk about the possibilities in vocations growing up. I think they just assumed we would all get married.

Catholic families need more information about the life of a priest or a sister. It seems that all the information that a lot of people receive is from the movies. Information not only about the dogma and the religion, but about the life of a priest, the life of a sister, what are the expectations. The day-to-day life is something that people generally do not know.

I homeschooled my daughter and used a Catholic curriculum and believe that made a huge impact on her. I also tried to make God part of my day, praying, reading, talking about God with my children. Talking about God's will in their life and to listen to what He wants them to do.

Contact with Priests and Religious

Finally, 7 percent of the religious order respondents and 11 percent of the family members said that families should facilitate contact with priests and religious for their children:

By making encounters with priests or religious, outside of church activities, possible—i.e., inviting them to dinner at home or special events, etc. In my opinion, this makes children realize that priests and religious are normal people just like us and that they lead happy, fulfilled lives.

I wish we had invited more Sisters to dinner. Growing up, we always had a priest over for dinner at least once a month. I wish we had extended that courtesy to the Sisters who we loved dearly.

Connecting me with priests and bringing up the issue more often.

Families can encourage vocations by becoming friends with priests and nuns. They can show the young that they are very normal and happy people.

CONCLUSIONS

Overall, the characteristics of families that nurture vocations to the priesthood or religious life are the same as those that nurture fervent and active lay Catholics and, for that matter, happy and healthy adults in all religious traditions. As the summary of major findings for the NRVC study put it, fostering happy and holy families is essential for nurturing vocations. The summary recommended:

- Pray daily as a family in thanksgiving, for guidance, and for forgiveness.
- Talk with your children about their worries and concerns, their hopes and dreams.
- Share meals together as often as possible.
- Tell stories about your family history—the good and the bad. Talk about how you became a family, and the day your children were born.
- Decide together your family goals and what your biggest do's and don'ts are.
- Be active in your parish and in your community. Encourage your children to participate in the ministries of the parish.
- Teach family members to fight fairly and forgive easily.
- Talk about your faith and the men and women, including sisters, brothers, and priests, who have had an important influence on you.
- Work to reduce stress among all family members. Have fun and play together each day.
- Encourage your children to be creative and compassionate and know that those are the greatest of God's gifts (Gautier, Wiggins and Holland, 2014).

4

The Influences of College Experiences on Religious Vocations

Thu T. Do

FOUR YEARS IN college seem to be too short a time to impact one's life vocational decision; however, they have proved to have a broad influence on an individual's life decision-making process. Among the many studies on the impact of college on students, a sizable number of studies explore comprehensively its impact on their life choice after graduation. Earlier researchers found that those who attended college were more likely than those who did not to understand public affairs, geography, history, humanities, and sciences (Pace 1979). They were less likely to rely on stereotypes in their judgments, more likely to be critical in their thinking, and more tolerant, flexible, and autonomous in their attitudes (Trent and Medsker 1968; Feldman and Newcomb 1969). Conducting a systematic review of the impact of attending college, Pascarella and Terenzini (2005) concluded that attending college had a significant impact on students. Students not only made statistically significant gains in factual knowledge and in a range of general cognitive and intellectual skills, but also developed a greater sense of interpersonal and intellectual competence, as well as a greater commitment to developing a meaningful philosophy of life.

In *Ex Corde Ecclesiae*, the papal document discussing the nature of the Catholic colleges and universities and presenting rules as well as guidelines for Catholic higher education institutions, Pope St. John Paul II wrote that Catholic colleges and universities participate in the mission of the Catholic Church by carrying out the pastoral ministry. Specifically, the Catholic university can assist students in "fostering vocations to the priesthood and religious life" (ECE 41). Thus Catholic colleges and universities are called to respond to this invitation by implementing initiatives that are unique as compared with other colleges and universities: continuing to teach philosophy and theology as required for undergraduate students, increasingly providing undergraduate majors and minors in Catholic studies, increasing the proportion of Catholic faculty, implementing Catholic research centers and institutes, and especially investing more in campus ministry programs (Yanikoski 2010).

Does college have an impact on student choice of a life vocation, particularly a religious vocation? Do the mentioned-above initiatives and programs at Catholic colleges and universities really impact students' religious vocational choices differently from non-Catholic colleges' and universities' programs? What are the differences between men and women on different influential aspects? This chapter examines the different aspects of college that may impact men's and women's religious vocational choices.

The chapter uses data from two major studies conducted by CARA: the first was a study of men religious and priests in 2012 (Cavendish, Cidade, and Muldoon 2012) and the second was a study of women religious in 2015 (Gautier and Gray 2015) in the United States. The chapter also includes findings from other CARA research on the impact of educational debt and vocations to religious life (Gautier and Cidade 2012).

CHARACTERISTICS OF NEW MEMBERS
Men in Priesthood and Religious Life

In 2012 CARA conducted a study to assess the role and influence of Catholic colleges and universities on the vocational discernment of men entering the seminary and religious life in the United States. A survey was sent to 5,246 men known and identified by Church leaders to be in formation or recently ordained. A total of 1,575 men (30 percent) completed the questionnaire. These respondents represented 46 seminaries, 84 religious institutes, and 109 dioceses across the United States. Two in five respondents (40 percent) are in some stage of formation for diocesan priesthood, 28 percent in formation for religious priesthood, 23 percent recently ordained diocesan priests, and 9 percent recently ordained religious priests.

The age range of respondents was from 19 to 68, with the majority in the 25- to 34-year-old age range. The average age was 33. Over four in five respondents (83 percent) were born in the United States, 2 percent were born in Canada or Europe, and 15 percent were born in other countries, mainly in Mexico, Vietnam, the Philippines, Colombia, and Nigeria. About nine in ten respondents became

Catholic as infants and their parents are Catholic, 5 percent when they were children or teenagers, and 7 percent when they were adults.

Nearly three in five (56 percent) respondents graduated from non-Catholic high schools, including public high schools (53 percent) and private high schools (3 percent). More than two in five attended Catholic high schools, including privately run (8 percent), diocesan-run (16 percent), and religiously run (22 percent) schools. Likewise, nearly three in five (56 percent) respondents graduated from non-Catholic colleges and universities, while two in five attended Catholic non-seminary colleges and universities, and 8 percent attended a Catholic seminary college for most of their college years.

Women in Religious Life

In 2014, CARA received funding from the Conrad N. Hilton Foundation for a study on the influence of college experiences on women's vocational discernment of religious life. CARA asked 209 new entrants, 114 newly professed, and more than 1,000 perpetually professed women religious who had entered religious life since 2000 in the United States to complete a survey of their experiences in college before entering their institutes and the impact these experiences may have had on their vocational discernment. A total of 883 surveys were completed. Among these participants, two in five (41 percent) respondents had professed their final vows, three in ten (32 percent) had professed their temporary vows, 14 percent were novices, and 13 percent were candidates/postulants.

On average, respondents entered their institutes in 2007, the average year of professing temporary vows was 2008, and the average year of professing perpetual vows among these respondents was 2014. Another 44 percent of the respondents anticipated professing perpetual vows after 2015. The respondents' average age was 37. The average age on entering the novitiate was 30. Of those who professed temporary vows the average age was 34. Of those who professed final or perpetual vows the average age was 43.

Eight in ten (79 percent) of the respondents were born in the United States, 9 percent were born in Asia or Oceania, 6 percent were born in Canada or Europe, 5 percent in Latin America, and 1 percent in Africa. Most respondents said they have been Catholic since infancy (87 percent). Seven percent became Catholic as a child or teen while only 6 percent converted to Catholicism as an adult. Eight in ten respondents (82 percent) reported that both of their parents were Catholic when they were teens. One in ten respondents had one Catholic parent and nearly one in ten (7 percent) said neither of their parents were Catholic.

A majority of respondents had attended public high school (53 percent), while 35 percent had attended Catholic high school, including 4 percent who had attended a school sponsored by a religious institute. Eight percent were home-schooled. During high school, three in ten respondents attended Mass more than once a week, and six in ten attended Mass once a week. More than half of the respondents had considered becoming a Catholic religious at least "somewhat" seriously prior to college. Nearly nine in ten respondents attended college before entering their religious institute. More attended public colleges than Catholic colleges (49 percent compared to 36 percent). Another 15 percent attended non-Catholic private colleges or universities.

INFLUENCES OF THE COLLEGE ENVIRONMENT ON VOCATIONS

Higher education institutions, especially Catholic institutions, have been attempting to help college students to recognize their life vocations while in college. But do their attempts really influence their students' decision to enter priesthood or religious life? This chapter explores the impact of the college environment on students' religious vocational discernment through the following aspects: the witnessed vocations by the presence of religious and priests on campus, academic courses, spiritual and devotional activities, service programs, and a campus climate that encourages or discourages students' religious vocational discernment. Specifically, this chapter pays attention to ways in which the activities and experiences of the men and women who attend Catholic colleges and universities are similar to or different from those who attend non-Catholic colleges and universities.

Witnessing Vocations

The data reveal that the likelihood of knowing a priest or religious depends on the type of campus. More than eight in ten men and women religious who attended Catholic colleges or universities had clergy or religious as a professor or campus minister in college (see Table 4.1). While few of those attending other non-Catholic campuses had professors who were clergy or religious, half of non-Catholic campuses did have clergy or religious as campus ministers.

CARA research indicates that knowing a priest or religious, and being inspired by their witness, has an impact on vocational choice. Men and women religious were asked to note the positive influence of clergy or religious as their professors and campus ministers on their vocational discernment. Men were more likely than

TABLE 4.1

Had a Priest, Sister, or Brother as a Professor or Campus Minister, by College Type

	Catholic Colleges		Non-Catholic Colleges	
	Men	Women	Men	Women
	%	%	%	%
Professors	89	83	17	8
Campus ministers	90	84	59	45

Sources: Data from Cavendish et al. (2012); Gautier and Gray (2015).

women to report that having clergy or religious as professors and campus ministers had a positive influence on their vocational discernment (66 percent and 55 percent for men compared to 27 percent and 38 percent for women). Among women, respondents who attended a Catholic college were more likely than those who attended non-Catholic colleges to report a positive influence of clergy or religious as their professors (71 percent for Catholic colleges compared to 29 percent for non-Catholic colleges) but were slightly less likely than those attending a non-Catholic college to report the positive influence of clergy or religious as their campus ministers (53 percent for non-Catholic colleges compared to 47 percent for Catholic colleges). Among men, respondents who attended Catholic colleges were more likely than those at non-Catholic colleges to report having a positive influence of clergy or religious as their professors and campus ministers on their vocational discernment.

In describing the influence that clergy and religious on campus had on their vocational discernment, most respondents referred to the personal witness of these individuals living out their vocation:

> *I had a religious sister who taught me during my freshman year of college and I remember being captivated by the fidelity of her lived religious life and wanting to know how she discerned her call. She shared her story with our class and this was definitely a beautiful witness to me at that time in my life.*

> *As a person pursuing a degree in biology in college, one of my biology professors who was a priest had a great influence on me. Through his example, I came to understand how God uses the gifts He gives His children.*

> *The priests at the two Catholic student centers I attended in my college years were extremely influential on my vocation. They were generous, prayerful men who were interested in the lives of the students under their pastoral care and were open to questions.*

Thu T. Do

I entered religious life—in large part—because of a religious brother who served
as a campus minister at my college. He was a tremendous role model for me, and a
reliable mentor. He walked with me through good times and tough times.

The presence of priests, religious sisters, and religious brothers on college
campuses was viewed as an important factor for those who later chose to follow
a vocation in the Church themselves. Results from the studies indicate that the
declining number of clergy and religious in the classroom and within campus
ministries would likely have a negative impact on the numbers of men and women
discerning a vocation in the future.

Participation at Mass

A majority of respondents indicated attending Mass at least weekly during college
(see Figure 4.1). However, this was more common among those attending Catholic
colleges and universities.

Among those who attended Catholic colleges, nearly all women reported
attending Mass weekly on campus while nine in ten men reported doing so. Men
and women attending non-Catholic colleges were less likely to indicate attending
Mass weekly or more often. This may be due to Masses being less available on
their campuses. Only 38 percent of women and 49 percent of men attending a non-
Catholic college reported that Masses were available on campus. Half of these men
and women attended Masses at a local parish during college.

Participants were asked to indicate the influence of Mass on their discernment of a religious vocation. This is evident on both Catholic and non-Catholic
campuses. In general, regardless of how often respondents attended Mass during

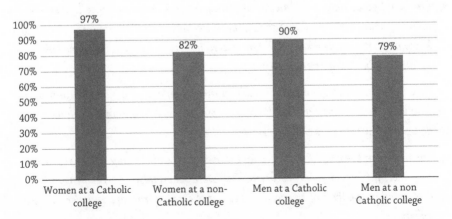

FIGURE 4.1. Weekly Mass Attendance during College
Sources: Cavendish et al. (2012); Gautier and Gray (2015).

college, about two-thirds or more considered this to have had at least "some" influence on their religious vocational discernment. However, both men (61 percent) and women (67 percent) attending Catholic colleges found their participation in Mass to have had "very much" influence on religious vocational discernment, more so than among those who attended non-Catholic colleges (45 percent for men and women).

Retreat Experiences

Two-thirds or more of the responding men and women took part in religious retreats while in college. In general, the women respondents were more likely than the men to participate in retreats (see Figure 4.2). Women at both Catholic and non-Catholic colleges are more likely than men to attend weekend or five-day retreats (91 percent for women compared with 59 for men). The same was true for religious retreats and one-day retreats. The most common sponsors for the retreats were campus ministry, followed by religious orders.

No matter how often they participated in retreats, three-fourths of men and women (76 percent) at both Catholic and non-Catholic colleges reported that retreats had at least "some" influence on their discernment of a religious vocation. Two in five respondents found retreats to have had "very much" influence on their discernment of religious vocation:

The retreats offered by campus ministry helped me to open up to my peers about my discernment, and made me realize that I not only had support from priests, but peers as well.

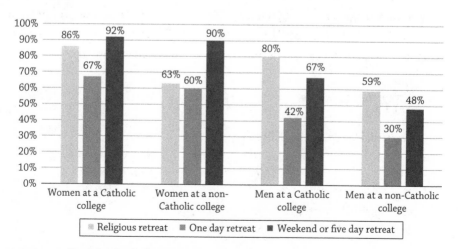

FIGURE 4.2. Participation in Retreats
Sources: Cavendish et al. (2012); Gautier and Gray (2015).

Attending retreats hosted by my community and held at the Motherhouse was probably the most influential thing in my discernment because it allowed me to see the sisters' way of life and to experience how much I felt at home here.

I had a strong moment in my life on a retreat that changed my outlook on life and from that moment on kept going back to that moment and still felt called to continue.

Retreat experiences through campus ministry gave me a chance to have a positive experience, then to continue to explore ministry in serving the same retreat years later. Authentic and meaningful conversations, both in where I was and from [the retreat director's] perspective.

Spiritual Direction

Respondents were also asked about their experiences of spiritual direction. Overall, men were more likely than women to have had a spiritual director while in college. Four in ten men had a spiritual director while three in ten women had one.

Among those who attended Catholic colleges, 62 percent of responding men said they had had spiritual direction during their time on campus (see Table 4.2). Women on Catholic campuses were less likely than men to report this, as were men and women respondents from non-Catholic campuses. The most common frequency for meetings with spiritual directors was monthly (63 percent for women and 62 percent for men). While this frequency was the same for women at both Catholic and non-Catholic colleges, men at non-Catholic colleges were less likely than men at Catholic colleges to meet monthly with their spiritual director.

The most common spiritual director was a diocesan priest or religious priest, followed by a religious sister (Table 4.3). Diocesan priests were more common at non-Catholic colleges than at Catholic colleges, while religious priests were more common at Catholic colleges. This may be due to the fact that more than 90 percent

TABLE 4.2

Spiritual Direction, by College Type

	Catholic Colleges		Non-Catholic Colleges	
	Men	Women	Men	Women
	%	%	%	%
Had a spiritual director	62	44	30	24
Met monthly	62	63	30	63

Sources: Data from Cavendish et al. (2012); Gautier and Gray (2015).

TABLE 4.3

Spiritual Director, by College Type

	Catholic Colleges		Non-Catholic Colleges	
	Men	Women	Men	Women
	%	%	%	%
Diocesan priests	35	24	50	50
Religious priests	57	51	42	20
Sisters	2	14	2	21

Sources: Data from Cavendish et al. (2012); Gautier and Gray (2015).

of Catholic colleges are currently sponsored by religious orders. Most priests currently ministering at non-Catholic colleges and universities are diocesan priests assigned by the local dioceses.

Among those who reported having had a regular spiritual director during college, almost all (94 percent) reported that having spiritual direction had at least "some" influence on their discernment of a religious vocation. There was little difference in terms of this influence between Catholic and non-Catholic colleges and universities. Nearly seven in ten respondents reported that spiritual direction had "very much" influence on their religious vocational discernment. This level of influence was reported less by women who attended Catholic colleges and universities than among those attending other campuses (60 percent compared to 78 percent); however, this level of influence was reported a little more by men who attended Catholic colleges and universities than those attending other campuses (67 percent compared to 62 percent):

A sister from the community of which I am now a member was my spiritual director for three years and she had a significant role as I would not be here as a religious today without her mentorship and guidance. She never pushed me but helped to guide me in seeking God's will.

One of the priests became my spiritual director and he really walked with me through the beginnings of discernment and my first few visits to the sisters.

Through the Newman Center I met sisters and learned what it meant to be a religious. One of the sisters who worked there often became my spiritual director and eventually my vocation director when I decided to enter her order. Mostly it was helpful to get to know sisters and have an example of what religious life looks like.

This priest was my spiritual director and professor in college. He was always ready to help me out when I needed spiritual advice.

TABLE 4.4

College Service Programs, by College Type

	Catholic Colleges		Non-Catholic Colleges	
	Men	Women	Men	Women
	%	%	%	%
Participation in service programs	78	76	63	51
Influence on religious vocation	61	65	59	55

Sources: Data from Cavendish et al. (2012); Gautier and Gray (2015).

College Service Programs

The survey respondents were asked if they had ever participated in any service programs during college. Nearly two-thirds of respondents indicated that they had participated in service projects during college. Once again, those who attended Catholic colleges were more likely than those at non-Catholic colleges to have been involved in service programs (see Table 4.4). Three in four of the respondents who attended Catholic colleges reported involvement in service projects and other campus ministry activities and programs, while three in five of those who attended non-Catholic colleges were involved in such programs.

Three in five respondents reported that the service projects had at least "some" influence on their religious vocational discernment, while 24 percent reported that their involvement in service projects had only a little influence on their vocational discernment. There were only slight differences in the influence of service programs on their vocational discernment among men and women at either Catholic or non-Catholic colleges/universities.

The most influential part of my vocational discernment was working with the people on the mission trips.

A couple of mission trips to Mexico with a group of peers and lay missionaries (Family Missions Company in Louisiana).

Devotional and Spiritual Practices

Respondents were also asked whether and how frequently they participated in various devotional and spiritual practices. More than two-thirds of respondents participated "at least" weekly in the practices shown in Table 4.5.

About eight in ten or more of those attending Catholic colleges prayed the rosary and participated in Eucharistic adoration while in college. Those attending

TABLE 4.5

Devotional and Spiritual Practices, by College Type (Percentage responding "at least weekly")

	Catholic Colleges		Non-Catholic Colleges	
	Men	Women	Men	Women
	%	%	%	%
Rosary	80	87	69	73
Eucharistic adoration	79	87	66	67
Liturgy of the Hours	67	71	48	44
Bible study	51	50	57	51
Lectio Divina	48	79	37	65

Sources: Data from Cavendish et al. (2012); Gautier and Gray (2015).

TABLE 4.6

Influences of Devotional and Spiritual Practices on Vocational Discernment, by College Type (Percentage responding "very much influence")

	Catholic Colleges		Non-Catholic Colleges	
	Men	Women	Men	Women
	%	%	%	%
Eucharistic adoration	54	73	51	54
Liturgy of the Hours	44	30	31	17
Rosary	34	33	31	32
Lectio Divina	29	35	25	33
Bible study	26	10	21	11

Sources: Data from Cavendish et al. (2012); Gautier and Gray (2015).

non-Catholic campuses were less likely to do so. Two-thirds of those on Catholic campuses prayed the Liturgy of the Hours weekly while fewer than half on non-Catholic campuses did so. About half of respondents participated in Bible study during college. This practice was just as common at non-Catholic colleges as on Catholic campuses. Women were significantly more likely than men to participate in other group prayer (80 percent for women compared with 15 percent for men).

Of these devotional practices, Eucharistic adoration had the most influence on the respondents' religious vocational discernment (see Table 4.6). Seventy-three percent of women at Catholic colleges said this practice had "very much" influence on their vocational discernment, as did 54 percent of women at non-Catholic colleges. Not as many men at Catholic colleges placed the same influence on Eucharistic adoration. Some 54 percent of men at Catholic colleges said it had "very much" influence on their discernment, compared to 51 percent of men attending non-Catholic colleges. Fewer, regardless of the type of college they attended, said that other devotional practices had "very much" influence on their vocational discernment:

> Adoration—I started stopping by the church for a few minutes on my way home from school. It was in the presence of the Blessed Sacrament that I heard the call, and received the courage to respond.

> It was a combination of daily Mass, daily rosary, and the encouragement of my closest friends. My vocation director also kept the process going.

> We also had opportunities for retreats, Eucharistic adoration, rosary groups, study groups to learn more about the Catechism of the Catholic Church, Bible studies along with times and trips for fellowship and service. The Newman Center became for me a home away from home.

> The support of a prayer life that I received in college was important but more important was the availability of Eucharistic adoration (permanently on campus) and the Mass (home parish was within walking distance during high school I attended daily; this habit I continued in college as was possible).

Campus Ministry

Respondents were also asked questions about whether there was a campus ministry on campus and how often they had participated in these activities there. Nine in ten respondents who attended Catholic colleges reported having had a campus ministry compared to two-thirds of respondents who attended non-Catholic colleges (see Table 4.7). Nearly two-thirds of respondents reported that they were engaged in service and social activities through campus ministry. Those who attended Catholic colleges were more likely to report having had Catholic campus ministry programs at the college they attended, and they were more likely than those who did not to have participated in these activities.

The availability of Catholic campus ministry programs on campus and participation in the social/service activities offered there had an impact on the respondents' religious vocation decision. Overall, one quarter of respondents stated that campus ministry had "very much" influence on their vocational discernment. There is little difference in response between those who attended a Catholic college and those who attended a non-Catholic college. Likewise, nearly a quarter of respondents

TABLE 4.7

Campus Ministry Programs, by College Type

	Catholic Colleges		Non-Catholic Colleges	
	Men	Women	Men	Women
	%	%	%	%
Catholic campus ministry program existed at the college	95	91	80	69
Participated in social activities sponsored by campus ministry	69	76	60	49
Participated in the service activities of campus ministry	58	76	43	51

Sources: Data from Cavendish et al. (2012); Gautier and Gray (2015).

reported that campus ministry programs such as social and service activities had "very much" influence on their religious vocational discernment.

College Roommates and Friends

The survey respondents were asked about their living arrangements on campus and whether they had had a roommate. Those who attended a Catholic college were more likely than those at non-Catholic colleges to have lived in a campus dorm and/or to have lived with roommates during college. Those who attended a non-Catholic college, on the other hand, were more likely to have lived off-campus or at home (Table 4.8).

Given the living arrangements, the level of influence of friends on the respondents' vocational discernment varied. Those who attended Catholic colleges reported their college friends had at least some influence on their vocational discernment, which is more than those at non-Catholic colleges reported (69 percent for men and 91 for women compared to 49 percent for men and 65 percent for women). Likewise, those at Catholic colleges (69 percent for men and 71 percent for women) received more support from their college friends than those at non-Catholic colleges (46 percent for men and 42 percent for women) for their vocational discernment.

The importance of peers in fostering and sustaining religious vocations should not be underestimated. Sociologists in general, and sociologists of religion in particular, have long recognized the importance of friendship networks in sustaining belief and practice. Peter Berger (1967) spoke of the importance of peer friendship

TABLE 4.8

Living Arrangement during College, by College Type

	Catholic Colleges		Non-Catholic Colleges	
	Men	Women	Men	Women
	%	%	%	%
Lived in a college dorm	84	86	74	65
Lived off-campus	54	31	66	54
Lived at home	23	18	42	42
Had a roommate	83	88	77	73

Sources: Data from Cavendish et al. (2012); Gautier and Gray (2015).

networks in terms of providing what he called "plausibility structures," which are the networks of like-minded others who help to sustain belief and commitment to things which might in other settings seem implausible to believe.

Discussion of Faith, Religion, and Prayer

Respondents were asked to report how often they discussed faith, religion, and prayer in the classroom and with various people outside of class during college. In general, women religious were more likely than men to frequently discuss faith, religion, and prayer while on campus. Those attending a Catholic campus were more likely than those at non-Catholic campus to frequently discuss faith, religion, and prayer (Table 4.9).

Men and women who attended Catholic colleges also reported frequent faith discussions in class (51 percent and 41 percent, respectively). Fewer men and women attending other campuses reported this (11 percent and 3 percent, respectively). Forty-three percent of men who attended Catholic colleges also reported frequent discussions about faith, religion, or prayer with professors outside of class. Women attending Catholic colleges were significantly less likely to report this (18 percent). Less than one in ten men and women attending non-Catholic colleges reported frequent discussions about faith, religion, or prayer with faculty outside of class (9 percent and 2 percent, respectively).

Vocational Discernment Programs

Respondents were asked if they had ever participated in any vocational discernment programs during college. Nearly half of all respondents participated in a "Come & See" event. Men and women respondents attending Catholic colleges

TABLE 4.9

"Frequently" Discussed Faith, Religion, and Prayer, by College Type

	Catholic Colleges		Non-Catholic Colleges	
	Men	Women	Men	Women
	%	%	%	%
With students outside of class	62	83	40	47
In class	51	76	11	12
With professors outside of class	43	48	9	10

Sources: Data from Cavendish et al. (2012); Gautier and Gray (2015).

TABLE 4.10

Participation in Vocational Discernment Programs during College, by College Type

	Catholic Colleges		Non-Catholic Colleges	
	Men	Women	Men	Women
	%	%	%	%
"Come & See" experience	58	65	45	38
Vocational discernment group	31	31	21	12
"Nun Run"/"Project Andrew"	8	12	8	8

Sources: Data from Cavendish et al. (2012); Gautier and Gray (2015).

were more likely than those on non-Catholic campuses to have attended "Come & See" events or live-in experiences with a religious order (Table 4.10). Fewer participated in a vocational discernment group during college, but again those at Catholic colleges were more likely than those at non-Catholic colleges to have had this experience. Only about one in ten or fewer participated in a "Nun Run" (for women) or "Project Andrew" (for men) while in college.

Participation in the various vocational discernment programs as mentioned above does influence individuals' vocational discernment. As more women religious participated in "Come & See" events, they were also more likely than men to report that such events had "very much" influence on their vocational discernment (72 percent for women, compared with 52 percent for men). Likewise, women religious were more likely to report that participation in a "Nun Run" had "very much" influence on their vocational discernment compared to men religious who had participated in "Project Andrew" (Table 4.11).

However, it is interesting to note that the influence of a vocational discernment group was stronger among women religious who attended non-Catholic colleges than it was among women who attended Catholic colleges. Women religious who

TABLE 4.11

Influences of Vocational Discernment Programs during College, by College Type (Percentage responding "very much influence")

	Catholic Colleges		Non-Catholic Colleges	
	Men	Women	Men	Women
	%	%	%	%
"Come & See" experience	51	76	53	69
Vocational discernment group	39	29	40	39
"Nun Run"/"Project Andrew"	18	53	22	44

Sources: Data from Cavendish et al. (2012); Gautier and Gray (2015).

attended a Catholic college were *less* likely than women religious who attended a non-Catholic college to report that their participation in a vocation discernment group had "very much influence" on their vocational discernment (29 percent compared to 39 percent).

Encouragement of Vocational Discernment While on Campus

The survey respondents were asked about who may have encouraged them to consider a vocation to religious life during college. The most common type of person mentioned was a friend, followed by professors, or a campus minister (Table 4.12).

Women who attended Catholic colleges were more likely than those who attended other campuses to have been encouraged by friends, religious sisters, campus ministers, parents, professors, religious brothers, siblings, and college staff. Men who attended a Catholic college were more likely than those who attended a non-Catholic college to have received encouragement to pursue a vocation from friends, professors, campus ministers, religious brothers, parents, and siblings.

When asked what kept them motivated in pursuing a vocation to religious life during college, men and women respondents shared different motivations in pursuing a vocation to religious life. Among women, the most frequent comments centered on a sense of being called by God, devotional practices, friends and family, as well as the culture and community of their college:

> *Frequent personal prayer, especially at Eucharistic exposition, a very strong Catholic family life, and the kind, encouraging letters I received from the vocations directress, all greatly helped me to pursue my vocation.*

TABLE 4.12

Encouragers of Vocational Discernment during College, by College Type

| | Catholic Colleges | | Non-Catholic Colleges | |
| | Men | Women | Men | Women |
	%	%	%	%
Friends	85	73	62	46
Religious sister	49	72	31	45
Professors	72	46	25	7
Campus ministers	58	45	46	28
Parish priest	74	42	69	39
Other	37	40	26	20
Religious brother	50	35	25	14
Parents	69	29	49	18
College staff	13	29	51	3
Siblings	59	24	39	13

Sources: Data from Cavendish et al. (2012); Gautier and Gray (2015).

I had a very strong group of Catholic friends to push and support me in all areas of my faith. This was also when I began to actually spend time just getting to know some religious sisters, and seeing how real they are was helpful.

The support of my friends, professors, and friends who were in religious life, especially young Jesuits who were friends of mine.

The constant array of spiritual activities made available by our campus ministry, from excellent retreats, to activities of all kinds being offered every day ("Supper Seminars," Adoration, Mass, the rosary, Bible studies, "Prayer & Praise," etc.) all helped me to pray more openly to the Lord every day and listen for what He had in mind.

Similarly among men, the most frequent comments centered on their personal prayer life, the example of a priest and/or religious, a sense of being called by God, a desire to serve God, the encouragement of friends, and their participation in the Mass:

Ultimately, the feeling in my heart that the priesthood was where I was to go. It kept resurfacing and I came to a point where I could not ignore it.

Good priests and nuns that lived out their vocation with joy and loyalty to the faith and the Church.

I was confident this was what God was calling me to do.

The desire to serve others and bring Christ's love to them.

Discouragement of Vocational Discernment while on Campus

Regardless of the type of college they attended, very few religious reported receiving any discouragement from other religious or from campus ministers or other college staff (Table 4.13). Respondents were more likely to recall being discouraged from discerning a religious vocation by their friends, parents, and siblings.

When asked what discouraged them from pursuing a vocation to religious life during college, men and women respondents differed in their recollection. Among men, the most frequent comments focused on the culture and environment of their college campus, other career ambitions or plans, women and dating, the requirement of celibacy, lack of support from family and friends, and the poor example of some priests, religious, and/or seminarians. Some respondents indicated that they were not yet discerning a vocation during their time as an undergraduate, so they reported that the question did not apply to them. Some respondents also identified issues facing the Church,

TABLE 4.13

Discouragers of Vocational Discernment during College, by College Type

	Catholic Colleges		Non-Catholic Colleges	
	Men	Women	Men	Women
	%	%	%	%
Friends	27	26	26	20
Parents	19	33	20	21
Siblings	14	22	11	17
Professors	13	11	12	12
Other	11	21	12	11
Campus ministers	7	4	3	2
College staff	7	6	7	5
Parish priest	5	3	5	5
Religious sister	4	9	2	2
Religious brother	2	<1	2	<1

Sources: Data from Cavendish et al. (2012); Gautier and Gray (2015).

including the clergy sex abuse scandal, as having discouraged their vocational discernment:

> *Giving up marriage and giving up other career opportunities that might not be possible as a religious.*
>
> *Celibacy and the sacrifice of not having children.*
>
> *The reaction of my family to my decision to enter seminary. They were very upset with me and tried many times to change my mind.*

Among women, the most frequent comments focused on family or friends discouraging them, desire for marriage and family, demands of social life and being a student, and their own fears or self-doubts:

> *What discouraged me the most were the people closest to me who kept discouraging me and telling me that I was too pretty to be a nun or that I would make a much better wife and mother than a religious sister. They put a lot of doubt into my heart.*
>
> *Some of my professors tried to persuade me to get a graduate degree before entering—which tempted my ambition—and I was also afraid that I might be making the wrong life choice in entering religious life.*
>
> *It was a pretty unknown path. I had some friendships with young men that I could have seen ripening into romance, and the idea of marriage was very attractive to me.*
>
> *My own lack of self-worth. I honestly believed I wasn't good enough or holy enough to be a sister. I had this notion that sisters were/are ultra-holy people who never sin. It was an unrealistic view of both sisters and myself.*

EDUCATIONAL DEBT

Another aspect that may impact men and women religious' discernment of a vocation to religious life is educational debt. In 2012, CARA conducted a study of the policies and practices of religious institutes in regard to educational debt in order to learn from the experiences of those institutes with inquirers and candidates who carry educational debt. A total of 477 religious institutes in the United States participated in the study. The findings revealed that religious institutes have experienced an increase in the number of inquirers who approach them with educational debt. The responding religious institutes were realistically cautious about encouraging the serious inquirers who approached them with educational debt.

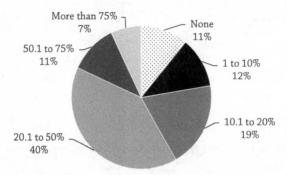

FIGURE 4.3. Percentage of Serious Inquirers with Educational Debt among Responding Institutes with at Least One Serious Inquirer
Source: Gautier and Cidade (2012).

On average, responding institutes with at least one serious inquirer in the last ten years reported that about a third of these inquirers (32 percent) had educational debt at the time of their inquiry. Of those institutes with at least three serious inquirers in the last ten years who had educational debt at the time of their inquiry, seven in ten turned away at least some inquirers because of their educational debt. On average, religious institutes with at least one formal applicant in the last ten years reported that a third of these applicants had educational debt at the time of their formal application, with debt averaging more than $20,000 (Figure 4.3). Slightly under half of the formal applicants with educational debt were eventually accepted into candidacy or postulancy.

The study also found that, given the educational debt, a number of men and women discerning religious vocation had to delay their application until they had paid or reduced their educational debt. Almost nine in ten responding religious institutes that had three or more inquirers with educational debt reported that they asked at least some of the serious inquirers who came to them with educational debt to delay their application because of the debt. The survey asked respondents if assistance with educational debt from others affected a candidate's freedom for continued discernment of his/her vocation. Superiors of religious institutes reported that educational debt tended to hinder candidates' discernment, and was especially likely to delay their decision to enter religious life.

Sometimes an inquirer will use an educational debt as an excuse for delaying discernment, even though this is not an issue for the congregation. Our current vocation director appreciates being able to remove the issue of delaying a decision by being able to state that arrangements can be made for the debt.

Yes, because candidates may have to delay longer to enter, and may change their minds.

One option is to delay an inquirer's entrance to candidacy but we continue to provide companionship and mentoring, guidance/assistance in the discernment process using a pre-candidate program. Another option is by extending the candidacy period, allowing the individual to stay in a formation convent with the candidate director with free board and lodging so the individual can pay off her loan.

Educational debt might delay entrance for those discerning a religious vocation. It also discourages men and women from even considering a vocation. Some religious communities suggest that candidates with high amounts of educational debt work in order to pay off or reduce it before entrance, but the delay may also discourage the candidates in their religious vocational discernment and cause them to reconsider their call to religious life.

CONCLUSIONS

Respondents reported that a variety of activities and experiences during their college years were influential in their religious vocational discernment. One of the most influential aspects of their college experience on their vocational discernment was participating regularly in spiritual direction. Respondents also rated a variety of vocation awareness and support programs, including "Come & See" events, as being influential in their vocational discernment. Other aspects of their college experience that were influential in vocational discernment included a variety of prayer and devotional practices such as Eucharistic adoration, Mass, and the rosary. The fact that Eucharistic adoration and Mass are centered on the Eucharist speaks of the importance that respondents assigned to the Eucharist in their own vocational discernment.

Clearly, spiritual direction, college retreats, and devotional practices on campus are important. Although campus ministries on non-Catholic campuses fulfill many of these elements, there appear to be greater opportunities and support available on Catholic campuses. Many of the factors that respondents reported as being influential in their vocational discernment are more available, more easily accessible, or more frequently practiced in Catholic colleges than in non-Catholic colleges. Compared to those who attended non-Catholic colleges, those who attended Catholic colleges were more likely to have a priest or religious as a professor, campus minister, or college administrator; to participate more frequently in spiritual direction, Mass, certain religious devotions, retreats, and service programs during college; and to report that the staff at their college expressed interest in faith, religion, and prayer. They were also more likely to report being encouraged in their vocational discernment by friends, professors, and campus ministry staff.

Those who attended non-Catholic colleges, on the other hand, matched or exceeded those who attended Catholic colleges in their participation in Bible studies, individual and group prayer, retreats of longer duration, and campus ministry leadership teams. When asked about the influence of various experiences on their vocational discernment, they were also as likely as those who attended Catholic colleges to assign "very much" influence to meeting regularly with a spiritual director during college, having a priest, sister, or brother who served as a campus minster; and participating in retreat experiences, campus ministry, and vocational discernment programs. They were also more likely than their counterparts at Catholic colleges to identify off-campus parishes as being highly influential.

The differences observed between those who attended a Catholic college and those who attended a non-Catholic college suggest that although Catholic college attenders were more likely to have been exposed to and participated in a wider array of activities and experiences that they report had fostered their vocational discernment, non-Catholic college attenders found support in discerning their vocation through participating actively in spiritual direction, campus ministry programs, retreats, vocational discernment programs, and off-campus parishes during college.

Although there are a small number of organizations that provide funds to assist candidates with educational debt, most responding religious institutes (or their candidates) did not receive funds from any of these sources. Educational debt is a challenge for discerners, for dioceses, and also for religious institutes. Interested candidates are too often turned away because of the educational debt, thus discouraging religious vocation. This barrier to vocations will likely increase as the extent of educational debt increases in society.

5

The Influences of Volunteer Programs on Religious Vocations

Patricia Wittberg

VOLUNTEERING IS VERY popular with teens and young adults today: Sixty-eight percent of Catholic teens and 45 percent of Catholic young adults report that they currently volunteer in some way or another. While most teenage volunteering is done locally, 43 percent of Catholic young adults have also volunteered in projects or programs outside of their own community (U.S. Conference of Catholic Bishops 2012). Tapping into this interest, many Catholic religious communities and colleges have begun offering extended, full-time volunteer opportunities that often last a year or more. Such programs often require the volunteers to live and pray together while working in a program that serves the poor—a lifestyle similar to that followed by many religious congregations of consecrated men and women. Young adults are most likely to participate in these live-in volunteer programs in the year immediately following their college graduation, but some Catholic colleges also have special residences on-campus where students can live together and commit to volunteering while pursuing their studies.

In addition to the many other factors explored in this book that might foster vocations to the priesthood or religious life, volunteer service programs may also do so. Surprisingly, however, the role of volunteer experiences in fostering religious vocations was almost completely neglected for many years. A single 2005 article in *Horizon*, the journal of the National Religious Vocation Conference, did discuss "discerning vocations through volunteer programs" (Medved 2005), but more than a decade passed before the topic was raised again. In 2016, a second

Horizon article described how the Alliance for Catholic Education Teaching Fellows Program at the University of Notre Dame (ACE) recruits between ninety and ninety-five recent college graduates each year to live in intentional communities while taking master's classes in education in the summer and teaching full-time in under-resourced Catholic schools during the academic year (del Fra 2016). Another article in the same issue discussed "the vocation impact of full-time volunteering" (Mulembe and Lackie 2016). Over ACE's twenty-two-year history, thirty-five ACE teachers have entered the priesthood or consecrated religious life, an entrance rate of 1.7 percent. This is a much higher percentage than for the overall Catholic population.

In addition to the study of ACE volunteers, a few studies of persons already in Church service also offer intriguing evidence that there may be some connection between volunteer programs and vocations. A study of Catholic high school teachers (Cook 2001) found that a steadily increasing percentage of the lay religion teachers in Catholic high schools have come from various Catholic volunteer programs. A CARA study of the influence of college experiences on women's vocational discernment to religious life (see Chapter 4 in this volume) noted in passing that, among the young women who had recently become sisters or nuns, over two-thirds had participated in some sort of volunteer program, and over half said that such programs had influenced their vocation decision (Gautier and Gray 2015:39). On the other hand, a recent Canadian study (Caudron and Rymarz 2013) found that the high school students who had volunteered in planning and leading retreats for their peers were *not* any more likely to become active adult Catholics later, let alone enter the priesthood or religious life. Some volunteer experiences, therefore, may be more likely than others to encourage vocations, and it would be important to know which ones.

Recently, the lack of studies on the connection between Catholic volunteer programs and vocations has begun to change. In 2013, the Catholic Volunteer Network (CVN) commissioned CARA to conduct an online survey of the alumni of all of its member programs. Subsequently, in 2014, the sponsors of one of these programs, DePaul University's Office of Mission and Values (OMV), asked CARA to conduct an online survey of "unaffiliated lay Vincentians": the young adults between the ages of 18 to 35 who had had a formative experience in the Vincentian mission either as a student or as a post-graduate volunteer. The latter survey was later expanded with four in-depth focus groups of former Vincentian volunteers, conducted in the spring and summer of 2015 in Chicago, New York City, and Denver. Each of these studies contains intriguing information on the connection between participation in a communal volunteer experience focused on prayer and service to the poor, and subsequent vocations to the priesthood and religious life.

CHARACTERISTICS OF THE VOLUNTEERS

Approximately three-fourths of the young adults who responded to the surveys were female.[1] This is a much higher percentage than the percentage of women in volunteer programs as a whole.[2] The vast majority (93 percent of the CVN survey) were white. The average age of the CVN respondents was thirty-seven, with one-third having volunteered prior to the year 2000. In contrast, the average age of the OMV respondents was younger (twenty-eight), and almost all had volunteered in more recent decades. Unlike the CVN respondents, all of whose volunteer experiences had occurred after their graduation from college, some of the OMV respondents had volunteered while still in college and living in special student houses with a volunteering focus.

Since different generations of Catholics often have different attitudes and behaviors, CARA divides Catholics into four generational categories: Pre-Vatican II (born before 1943), Vatican II (born between 1943 and 1960), Post-Vatican II (born between 1961 and 1981), and Millennial (born after 1981).[3] Forty-four percent of the respondents to the CVN survey were members of the Post-Vatican II generation and 41 percent were members of the Millennial generation. In the OMV survey, 81 percent of the respondents were Millennials and only 19 percent were from previous generations. In both surveys, therefore, the respondents were much younger than the Catholic population as a whole, of whom only 36 percent are of the Post-Vatican II generation and 15 percent of the Millennial generation.

Forty-seven percent of the respondents to the CVN survey were married; 42 percent had never married. As might be expected from their younger average age, only 25 percent of the OMV respondents were married, while another 21 percent described themselves as being in a committed relationship.[4]

Experiences before Volunteering

The respondents were much more likely than the average Catholic to have had a Catholic education: Forty-four percent of the CVN respondents had gone to a Catholic grade school, 43 percent to a Catholic high school, and 58 percent to a Catholic college. Sixty-eight percent of the OMV respondents reported receiving their undergraduate degree from a Catholic college or university; 42 percent

---

[1] The percentage female for the CVN survey was 72 percent; for the OMV survey it was 78 percent.
[2] Women comprise 51 percent of the U.S. population, and 58 percent of all those who volunteer in the U.S.
[3] Refer to Chapter 3 for a fuller description of these categories.
[4] The category "in a committed relationship" was not included in the CVN survey, but 6 percent of the CVN respondents did say they were "living with a partner," which may mean the same thing.

had even received their graduate degrees from a Catholic institution. This was a higher percentage than the percentage of Catholics as a whole who have attended Catholic schools. In general, the respondents were more highly educated than the average Catholic: Approximately 40 percent had completed their BA degree, while 57 percent (CVN survey) or 49 percent (OMV survey) had also completed a graduate degree. Most had not worked full-time prior to participating in the volunteer program.

Approximately 80 percent of the respondents to both surveys had been raised as Catholics, and most had remained Catholic during their volunteer experience. However, only about two-thirds of the CVN survey respondents claimed to be still Catholics. This is approximately the same as the retention rate of persons raised Catholic in the United States as a whole. Millennial respondents to the CVN survey were less likely than those from older generations to say that their present religious identity was Catholic (62 percent as compared to 71 percent of the Post-Vatican II respondents). In the OMV survey, of the 266 respondents whose childhood tradition was Roman Catholicism, 84 percent remained Catholic. Since the OMV respondents' volunteer experiences were more recent than those of many CVN respondents, it remains to be seen whether their retention rate will also fall in future years.

The Volunteer Experience

Almost all (94 percent) of the CVN respondents had participated in an established volunteer program for nine months or longer. Most (80 percent) had served in the United States; another 11 percent had served in Central or South America. Over half (55 percent) of the CVN respondents had volunteered in the Jesuit Volunteer Corps or the Jesuit Volunteer Corps Northwest. Other large programs, counting altogether for an additional 21 percent of the volunteers, were the Notre Dame Mission Volunteers, the Christian Appalachian Project, the Mercy Volunteer Corps, the Lasallian Volunteers, the Friends of the Orphans, and the Maryknoll Lay Missioners. In all, the CVN respondents had volunteered in a total of 59 different programs.

Almost all (93 percent) of the CVN respondents had lived in community with other volunteers during their time of service. On average, the CVN survey's respondents had lived with six other volunteers while serving in their program. Just over three quarters (77 percent) of the CVN respondents said that they had regular, structured prayer or reflection times while in the program. This percentage was higher for the more recent volunteers than for the ones who had volunteered before the year 2000. All of the OMV respondents reported living together and praying together at structured prayer times while in their volunteer program.

Most of the CVN respondents reported receiving a stipend (91 percent), room and board (89 percent), and medical insurance (74 percent) during their year of service. Four in ten said that their program also offered an educational loan deferment, while about one-third were given travel expenses. Almost half (47 percent) said that their placement had been in education, while another 40 percent had volunteered in a social service placement.

THE RELIGIOUS IMPACT OF THE VOLUNTEER EXPERIENCE
Development of a Strong and Active Catholic Laity

The first step to increasing the number of vocations to the priesthood or religious life is to foster the development of a strong and active laity from which these vocations would come. Both the CVN and the OMV surveys, as well as the four focus groups, asked the respondents about their current Catholic practice. The studies found that the survey respondents were more likely to report regular religious service attendance and frequent prayer than either American Catholics overall or the general U.S. population (see Table 5.1). Male former volunteers in the CVN study were more likely than female former volunteers to say they attend religious services at least once a week today (50 percent as compared to 44 percent).

The participants in the focus groups also agreed that their experiences of prayer and community during their volunteer time period had led them to greater involvement in their parish or faith community. At least one person—usually more than one—in each focus group was currently employed in university campus ministry. Several others were actively involved as parishioners in their parishes.

> *Yeah, I'm very close to the church that I currently go to. And that's very important to me and I don't have any intention of not being connected to a church congregation.*
>
> *Same for me.*

In addition to praying and attending religious services more often than other Catholic adults, the CVN respondents also indicated a higher level of participation in other activities within their parishes. Such activities included parish-sponsored community service, fellowship/social activities, family activities, faith/Bible discussion groups, youth/young adult programs, religious education programs, choir, and the like. The CVN respondents were almost three times more likely than the average Catholic to serve on their parish council or other committees. They were

TABLE 5.1

Religious Practice among Former Volunteers, Compared to U.S. Catholics and
the U.S. Population

	CVN Study* %	OMV Study* %	U.S. Catholics %	U.S. Population+ %
Attendance at religious services				
More than weekly	13	**	4	8
Once a week	33	71	21	19
Two/three times a month	14	15	5	4
About monthly	12	10	20	16
A few times a year or less	28	7	50	53
Frequency of prayer				
Several times a day	33	43	22	27
Once a day	21	24	37	29
Several times a week	21	25	11	12
Once a week	7	4	11	7
Less than once a week	18	1	12	11
Seldom/never	–	3	51	14

Sources: * CVN statistics include respondents who were not Catholic (17% of the total); OMV statistics
include only Catholic respondents; ** the OMV study combined "more than weekly" and "once a week"
in one category; + Data from the 2012 General Social Survey; all CVN data from Saunders, Gaunt, and
Coll (2013); all OMV data from Saunders, Coll and Gaunt (2014).

more than twice as likely to participate in faith-sharing groups. Still, as one participant noted, very few young adult Catholics are in these kinds of lay leadership
positions. Their own involvement in such activities is counter-cultural in comparison with others of their peers, and they worried about what this lack of involvement meant for the life and vitality of parishes in the future:

I have a home parish in which I am very involved. . . . We see that as one of our
responsibilities, looking around and seeing very few people in our age brackets
saying, "This is going to be us." When you look at the parish council, which we are
not on. In ten or fifteen years, that's going to be us. We are going to be the ones who
are still around. I feel very fortunate that I have this—it is also the parish that
I grew up with. I am very fortunate that I have this connection.

I'm kind of fearful, in looking at the future, in looking at getting married and
having a family. Because when I grew up we had a really connected parish. You
want this family formation, and we had a lot of that and it was awesome. And now
I look at churches and I don't see them being so active, in activities for the families,

and catechesis, and youth programs, and social activities. . . . It doesn't mean I'm not going to go to church or anything like that, but I'd like to see that in the future for our parishes.

Former volunteers also reported other types of volunteering and support for religious organizations outside of the parish. Former volunteers in the CVN survey are almost twice as likely as the U.S. population overall to volunteer for all types of causes. They are also more likely than other Catholics overall to volunteer or donate money to religious organizations, or than the U.S. population as a whole. The average overall amount of money given to religious organizations by the Catholic former volunteers in the past twelve months was $2,282. This compares to $1,664, the amount that respondents of other religious preferences gave in the past twelve months. The Catholic CVN respondents are more likely than other U.S. Catholic adults to be involved in a home parish or to participate in faith-sharing groups, although—perhaps because of their comparative youth or the demands of early parenthood—they are less likely to be in leadership roles as parish council or committee members. Sixty-eight percent of the CVN volunteer alumni say that their volunteer year experience was either "somewhat" or "very" important in their later decisions to donate or volunteer (Table 5.2).

TABLE 5.2

CVN Alumni Actively Involved in Volunteering and Giving, Compared to U.S. Catholics and the U.S. Population

	CVN Study %	U.S. Catholics %	U.S. Population %
Percentage actively involved in			
Home parish (Catholics only)	69	59[**]	54[**]
Parish council or committee member	6	17+	−
Faith-sharing groups	34	15+	−
Volunteering for religious organizations	49	41[*]	51[*]
Donating money to relig. organizations	64	55[*]	64[*]
Volunteering (all types)	77	57[*]	66[*]
Donating money (all organizations)	83	79[*]	84[*]
How important was the volunteer year in later decisions to donate or volunteer?			
Somewhat important	40	−	−
Very important	28	−	−

Sources: [*] Gallup (December 13, 2013); [**] Kosmin and Keysar (2006:58); + D'Antonio, Dillon, and Gautier (2013:118); all CVN data from Saunders, Gaunt, and Coll (2013).

Searching for a Spiritual Home

The former volunteers valued the intense experiences of prayer and community they had enjoyed during their year of service, but they noted that it was often difficult to find similar experiences in other Church settings afterward. Almost all focus group participants described a period of "parish shopping" which, for some, had not yet ended:

Finding a church is really difficult because another thing [the volunteer placement] does is it heightens your expectations. It heightens your expectations of what spirituality and relationship should look like. And so you go into some of these, which I think all of us do, traditional Catholic churches and sometimes those experiences can feel very inauthentic. And when you feel that, I push away from that.

It's difficult. I consider myself to be quite a Church-hopper in the last four years. The parish that I went to before I came to St. John's doesn't really feel like home anymore. . . . I look around. I have been active and looking to find a place where I want to go to Mass, but there hasn't been a place where I really feel called to join in a real parish way where I am participating in the Mass itself, getting involved in service projects. It is difficult, and I am still looking.

You can still go to the [student] Mass. There's that feeling, "I graduated. Should I be here?" So, it's that awkward feeling. Am I just holding onto something that I did in college that I need to let go of? And then, to go to the [other] Mass, it's all neighborhood people. I don't know anyone. It's all people with children and babies and older people. So you don't really fit into the college community but you also don't fit into the neighborhood community either. Finding that in between space has been hard for me.

It was very important to the participants that they feel a sense of community in any parish they attended. Many expressed a sense of social anxiety about entering a situation where they didn't know anyone; others noted that being the only representative of their age cohort in a parish felt lonely and disconcerting:

Participant: *I'm not connected with a church of my choice in Denver, but I go to church with my grandparents at times. It's their church and it's not exactly what I would choose, but it's the only time I get to spend time with them. And I enjoy spending time in that community, which is so important to them. It sounds kind of silly, maybe, not to engage in what I want, what I would choose. But for me, going* to church by myself seems less fun than going to church with my grandparents and engaging in that relationship with them.

Facilitator: *Is that a problem, going to a church by yourself?*

Participant: *Yes.*

Participant: *It sucks (Laughter).*

Participant: *Once you meet people, make connections. Like, now the church where I go, there are friends there and yeah it's, it's not a problem at all. But if you're going to a new church, where you're just going by yourself, that's when it's not happening.*

Volunteering and Life Choices

Almost all of the CVN respondents agreed that their volunteer service year had made them better, more compassionate persons. Almost all (97 percent) also either "somewhat" or "strongly" agreed that their volunteer program experience "helped me become who I am today." Among the CVN respondents, two-thirds said that their volunteer service was either "somewhat" or "very" important in their choice of a career, and six in ten said it was "somewhat" or "very" important in their vocational/faith development discernment process. The female CVN respondents were more likely than the male respondents to say that their volunteer service was "very" important in influencing their choice of career (45 percent compared to 40 percent). Among the OMV respondents, 88 percent either "somewhat" or "very much" agreed that their relationship with the Vincentian mission in their volunteer experiences had strongly influenced their career and life decisions. Over half of the OMV respondents who were married or in a committed relationship stated that their Vincentian experience had influenced their relationship with their spouse or partner.

Reflecting the survey findings, several participants in the focus groups also mentioned that they had changed their career plans after their college or post-college Vincentian volunteer experiences. A few participants, while not changing careers, had nevertheless developed specific preferences for the kind of organization where they wished to practice their career, or the attitude they developed toward the people they served or worked with:

It really helped me to understand the Vincentian mission of service and justice and kind of took me from a place where I felt like with my communication degree I was highly qualified to be a secretary or a housewife, and then I felt like after that I could see a path of social service work that could lead me down. So that was what led me to do the second volunteer experience that I did at Mercy Home and that is what then led me to pursue a career in social services.

I went back to a place to work where I would get to live out that Vincentian approach to work and service, wanting to come back to Chicago, I knew that there were very few organizations that I was willing to come back and work for. A huge part of that was that I wanted it to be connected to the Vincentian mission somehow.

I like to think that I bring some dignity to the banking world. [Laughter] Just a little bit, especially when my manager is ready to kick someone out because they're negative four or five hundred dollars instead of helping them try to find a solutions. I'm just like, "No. We can do this. We'll figure this out. I'm going to call the social worker, because [the bank's client] can't communicate with me or you. And you're just frustrated so that's why you're kicking them out, not because we don't have a solution for them." . . . I feel like I wouldn't have the backbone to—or the facts and figures or experience behind me—if I hadn't seen what I saw in the Vincent and Louise House.

Volunteering and Religious Vocations

Former volunteers are much more likely than the average Catholic adult to say that they have considered a vocation to ordained ministry or religious life. This is especially true for male volunteers (Table 5.3). Those who had considered a vocation were also much more likely to have done so seriously: More than three in

TABLE 5.3

Alumni Consideration of a Religious Vocation, Compared to U.S. Catholics			
	CVN Study	OMV Study	U.S. Catholics*
	%	%	%
Percentage responding "yes"			
Have you considered a vocation to ordained ministry or religious life?	37		—
Females only	31		15
Males only	54		17
Have you ever considered a vocation to . . . religious life or ordained ministry in any faith?		46	
Females only		42	
Males only		64	

Source: * Data in this column from Gray and Perl (2008); all other data from Saunders, Gaunt, and Coll (2013); Saunders, Coll, and Gaunt (2014).

five of the CVN respondents (62 percent) and over half (56 percent) of the OMV respondents have considered religious life or the priesthood either "somewhat" or "very" seriously. Again, it was the male volunteers who were much more likely than the women to say they had seriously considered a vocation. Millennials were more likely than the Post-Vatican II generation to say they had considered a vocation, according to the CVN survey, but less likely, according to the OMV survey, to say they had done so seriously.

For 6 percent of the CVN respondents, these early considerations have already led to a vocation as an ordained priest, seminarian, deacon, or religious—again, a far higher percentage than average for U.S. Catholic adults.

Only one participant in the focus groups was actively discerning a call to religious life. Several of them had considered a vocation in the past, and many knew of other volunteers who had done so:

During my [volunteer placement] year, like, there were three women, including myself who were discerning religious life and at least one guy who was discerning religious life.

During my year there was one girl, but she didn't really share that with anyone until afterwards I found out. I think she, like, continued to immerse herself [in discernment].

One of our friends who went here and is a recent grad did his bachelor's and master's here has just signed away to enter the Vincentians, so that's exciting. That just happened recently, so that's the first person that comes to mind.

The volunteers' increased likelihood of considering a religious vocation may be due in part to the fact that volunteer programs seem disproportionately to attract young adults who were already thinking of the possibility that they might be called to the priesthood or religious life. The CVN survey found that over three-fourths of its respondents said they had considered a vocation to the ordained ministry or religious life prior to their volunteer service. Close to half continued to do so during and after their service as well.

In the focus groups, several participants mentioned that they had been thinking about a vocation prior to their service year, and that they appreciated the opportunity for discernment offered by the volunteer program, even if they ultimately decided not to become a priest, brother, or sister:

I considered religious life from the time I was in high school to a little over a year ago, on and off again. [The volunteer placement] for me was, it was very private for me. It was hard for me to talk about, even with people who were part of my community or really close friends. But, [the volunteer placement] did give me an opportunity to do a lot of intention around that, to do some reading. And my spiritual director that year was a sister, so, I had the opportunity to talk to her about that and to really do some intentional journaling. So, [the volunteer placement] was really supportive in that way, even though it didn't know it was being supportive, by just providing like a safe place to kind of think about it.

Even though none of the focus group participants had decided to enter religious life as yet, several had entered Church service as lay ministers, either at a parish or with the campus ministry program at the university they had formerly attended:

I've been blessed to work in a church now, [and] we have Mass every day. I come to work every day in an office with 20 people. I'm blessed. Not many people get to do that. So it's definitely been a gift in my life. . . . I'm just thankful God put me in a place where I can let that grow in my life, and I'm not ashamed to say that. I like my religion. I enjoy being Catholic and it's a great gift in my life.

Although I didn't necessarily say that I had the intention of becoming a campus minister or work[ing] at St. John's, because I had known the charism so well, it made me feel like I was home in a real way. Making that transition, it's been a wonderful transition, of being someone receiving the mission to someone who is an agent of that mission, a co-worker with the Vincentians and the Daughters of Charity and the other lay Vincentians here.

After the Volunteer Year

What about the other 94 percent of former volunteers who have not entered religious life or the ordained priesthood, especially the 22 to 27 percent who had once "very seriously" considered doing so? How did they attempt to retain and foster the lessons of their volunteer experience in their post-volunteer lives? Most (77 percent) of the CVN respondents said that they had remained in regular or occasional contact with fellow volunteers after their year was completed. Women were more likely to remain in regular contact with their fellow volunteers than men were (45 percent as compared to 33 percent). Among the OMV former volunteers, close to three-fourths (70 percent) "strongly" agreed that they remained in regular contact with each other, while almost all (96 percent) at least "somewhat" agreed. In fact, over four in ten (44 percent) said that they continued to volunteer for a Vincentian group or organization; approximately one-third were involved in Vincentian prayer, faith sharing, or formation groups (37 percent) or contributed financially to the support of Vincentian ministries (30 percent). Among the CVN respondents, 13 percent said they continued to volunteer with the program where they had served their volunteer year.

A desire for present-day community and service experiences similar to those they had had in their volunteer service was also the most commonly cited desire among the focus group participants. They were unanimous in stating that the friendships they had formed during their volunteer experiences are still their most valued friendships today. Several also noted that they had met and formed relationships with persons they would never have befriended otherwise, and that these diverse friendships had enriched their lives:

I might be just still coming off my [volunteer program] high, but I don't associate— like, I have co-workers—but I don't associate with people that don't have the Vincentian background. [Laughter] I don't have close friends that didn't go to DePaul or didn't live with me.

I have made great friends with people, who if I had met them through something outside the Vincentian, probably would not be friends. I would maybe put up with them, socialize with them, but you know it just kind of brings you together in a different way.

The participants noted that their previous Vincentian friendships were useful in networking when arriving in a new city, and also helped them share their joys and frustrations. This was especially true for some of the Denver participants, who were somewhat older than those in the other focus groups and had worked longer in demanding social service professions:

That's exactly how I made my first friend in Denver when I moved here too. A girl I volunteered with connected me with another girl who lives here from another year in my program and we're closest friends now because we have that bond or that realization of sharing it with something larger than yourself.

And then, in this community. Like, this is home for me. Because I can share about the struggles, here. . . . Sometimes, to serve the poor is really hard. But I can share, share that struggle here, where I can't share that struggle elsewhere, because I know the people here love those people as I do.

The role of community in prayer was another characteristic of their volunteer experience that the focus group participants had attempted to replicate:

> I think that it is so easy to find the volunteer opportunities. I think that it is difficult to find the intentional prayer opportunities. That takes a lot commitment and trial and error, sometimes, especially after graduating.

> For me, it is the community prayer and really just the conversation and awareness of issues. . . . Praying for things that not everyone is necessarily praying about and for and having that kind of mindset. That's just me; don't get me wrong, having those service opportunities would be really great too, but for me it's really the community and prayer.

The former volunteers stated that they would like to become more involved in volunteering, prayer, and community with other former volunteers: Among the OMV respondents, three-fourths (74 percent) wanted to be more involved with Vincentian community outreach or volunteer programs, while over half were interested in participating in faith-sharing or prayer groups, organized social activities, or outreach to youth and children. Half were "very" interested in learning about opportunities for short-term mission projects. Serving with a community of others who share the Vincentian mission and values when making life choices was at least "somewhat important" to almost six in ten (57 percent) of the OMV survey respondents. Millennial respondents seemed to have been more interested than older respondents in finding ways to remain involved in future service opportunities. The focus group respondents agreed:

> I would love if there was some kind of group to join, but not necessarily affiliated with [University] specifically . . . something bigger than that, with a larger Vincentian connect, but there kind of isn't. That would be great, and a lot of my friends and family would be interested in that.

> With today's technology, it would be nice to have some [kind] of central alumni or current volunteer network or cloud-based system to connect and share. This [could be some sort of] communal blog and you can find people. At least that's a good way to find community again and create opportunities again and connect.

> Yeah, a lot of people want to have these [service] experiences. One of the great things I did was, I did a program sponsored by Franciscan sisters in Central America. It was as a global awareness through experience. It was great. So I went to Guatemala for ten days and I didn't do any volunteer work. I met people and heard

people's stories. I learned about what was going on there, and really witnessed a thirty-year tragedy that had happened there. So experiences like that, where you provide people an opportunity, within the confines of their job when all they can get is a week off work. And just be in solidarity with people, learn from people, listen to people, live with people. Rather than building a house or a church or a pre-school. Those are the kinds of international experiences I've taken the most from. You could have it has a domestic experience as well.

[Something to] connect all those people under one umbrella, to have a social aspect, a prayer aspect, a service aspect to kind of keep in motion all of the formation that we've had as students at [University] or as people who have done service programs, to kind of keep that moving after the college or post-grad service has ended.

Barriers to Involvement

Respondents to both surveys, as well as the later focus group participants, listed several factors that hindered them from increasing their involvement. Lack of time was the most frequently mentioned: Over half (57 percent) of the CVN respondents cited time as a barrier, more than all of the other cited reasons put together. "Catering to busy people working full time" was one of the most widely mentioned answers to the open-ended question in the OMV survey on how the Vincentian programs could better address the needs of former volunteers, and was a frequently raised problem in the focus groups as well.

We constantly get questions of, "Oh, what do you have for alumni?" But to your point, sometimes we will plan things and people will say, "Oh, that's such a great idea, but I can't make it." Or "How about you plan this . . . " and then we go plan it, and they're not able to make it. The reality of what people are able to do versus— I know they love that connection, but I don't know what would bring people to-gether. It has to be very easy to come to and be involved in. We haven't figured it out yet, but I definitely hear that a lot.

I kind of wonder if, because so many of our alumni get hired on to the places where they were working, or go to school, or work in ministry. And in any of those scenarios you have a really weird schedule. And so if you're working in a hospital and you work overnight, or if you're going to school and you have classes and a job, or if you have four kids. That's not to say it's not a great program, but I think just the circumstances of where people end up after a year like this is they're strapped for money and they're strapped for time.

Other former volunteers cited the difficulty of finding suitable opportunities, especially if they had moved some distance away from the Vincentian university they had previously attended, or from the service opportunities they had previously been involved in:

> Even just listening to this, it feels like sometimes if people go places, if there is a way for people to know how to connect. . . . It's disheartening a little bit. How do you just let people who are interested know who to connect with? Do you have to find a St. Vincent DePaul society? Do you have to find the Daughters? Where do you go?

> I was bored the other day, and I went on the St. Vincent DePaul society website to see where they have chapters in [the state the participant is moving to], and they're all on the other side of [the state]. It's like a four- or five-hour drive from where I will be.

> And it's harder to stay connected when you don't live in the same place with people that I shared that experience with.

Implications for Religious Institutes

One of the *Horizon* magazine articles mentioned at the beginning of this chapter noted that, while volunteers frequently contemplate a religious vocation during their time of service, very few enter religious life immediately after their volunteer year is over (Mulembe and Lackie 2016). More typically, they go back home and work for a few years while they try to assimilate what they have learned. Many would like help in their reflection and discernment. As several of the focus group participants put it:

> I kind of feel that in my experience of being a Vincentian, it kind of undid a lot of my early teaching of my religion. . . . I was still in the middle of that when I was graduating, and I haven't managed to tie the loose ends back up. So I feel like I probably could have used some—I'm three, four years out now and I'm still trying to tie up some loose ends. I can't go home. I can't go back to where I was, but I need to figure out where I'm moving forward to. So that's something that would be helpful.

> I think being in your early to mid-20s is a moment in which you are becoming an adult, figuring out who you are. I am not really sure the kind of person I would have been had I not chosen to do service work. Maybe I would have been a fine person.

I am sure I wouldn't have been a terrible person. [Laughter]. But my life would not have been the way that I interact with people and talk to people. The choices that I make and what I buy and what I do, would be very different if I hadn't had that lens handed to me at the age of 22, which was older than a lot of other people even. Even if I never did volunteer work again, I would still be a Vincentian. You kind of can't shake it once you have that lens placed in front of you.

To meet this desire for discernment and reflection, the *Horizon* article's authors maintained that it is important for religious institutes to explore ways of "developing friendships with volunteers during their time of service and keeping the door open during the years afterward" as they continue their discernment process. Otherwise, as several focus group participants noted, the memory of the volunteer experience fades and becomes less salient in their lives:

I have [a] part-time job and a graduate assistantship, and between all of that I don't have a lot of extra time, and I find myself naturally moving into new communities with people that I am working with every day. A lot of that strong sense of Vincentian connection goes away a little bit.

I majored in Catholic Studies here at [university] and was very involved here in Catholic Campus Ministry. I spent a lot of time at church and on retreats. Also part of it is that now where I am at, a lot of people I am around have been really negatively impacted by the Church. . . . So there's a lot of people who are sort of trying to figure out what their relationship is to it. I wouldn't say that I've lost it, but I am in that space where I don't know what I think about it all.

Unfortunately, religious institutes have often been slow to connect with volunteers or volunteer alumni. The CVN survey asked its respondents how they had learned about the volunteer program they had joined. Approximately one-third (35 percent) learned about it through their friends, and another one-third (31 percent) through their college campus ministry office. Fewer than 5 percent learned about their program from local clergy, and fewer than 2 percent from a male or female religious. The authors of the *Horizon* article noted that many, if not most, religious institutes do not have the resources to begin and run their own volunteer programs, although a recent grant from the Conrad N. Hilton Foundation is providing financial assistance to sixteen women's religious institutes to begin such initiatives. Equally important are efforts to provide post-volunteer experiences for former volunteers whose lives were profoundly changed by their service year and who are now discerning what to do next.

The former volunteers themselves are asking for more opportunities to preserve or re-establish the sense of community and purpose they had experienced during their volunteer experience. When the OMV survey asked its respondents to finish the sentence "The Vincentian Family can better address my needs by . . . " over half of the respondents gave suggestions. Of the seventeen main themes that appeared in their answers, five reflected a desire for opportunities to live the Vincentian spirit and values in their present lives,[5] and another five reflected a desire for accessible Vincentian service opportunities. Some of the individual responses to the OMV survey included sentiments like the following:

> Are there any opportunities available for former volunteers to form community and live together once they leave a Vincentian program? Since leaving it has been difficult to find a house arrangement and roommates that replicate the community life and commitment to service and simple living.

> [The Vincentian family can better meet my needs by] being more involved with my life after I have completed my year of service. I gained so much knowledge and passion while I was serving, but now it has just dropped off the edge.

Similar sentiments surfaced in the focus groups:

> I have been pestering the [Religious Institute] for the longest time to form a lay affiliate group. I know a lot of different groups of sisters have lay groups that are just connected to them, where you can go and eat dinner and pray and serve and all that wonderful stuff.

> And so, as someone who's very passionate about the charism and finds a lot of life in the charism and in this family, I think it would be really valuable to either start some sort of community for young adults, so that we can grow into it and keep this charism alive or to look at the structures we already have like the St. Vincent DePaul Society and really just analyze and assess what are we doing, who are we, how are we living out this Vincentian charism.

> [I would like] a way to commit yourself organizationally to the charism and in a way that is not necessarily being done now.

---

[5] "Connecting me to local Vincentians," "Communicating and sharing updates about Vincentian work," "Providing accessible Vincentian material for ongoing faith formation," "Replicating the Vincentian sense of community in my local area," and "Enabling young leaders in the Vincentian family."

In addition to setting up structures and opportunities for former volunteers to become involved in, it would also be important for individual religious themselves to develop personal relationships as friends or mentors with the former volunteers. According to the OMV survey, over half (52 percent) of the former volunteers consider other lay volunteers "very much" their mentors in learning about and living out the Vincentian mission. In comparison, far smaller percentages considered vowed religious such as the Daughters of Charity (34 percent) or the Vincentian priests (28 percent) to be mentors in this way. Establishing an ongoing contact with former volunteers could therefore be beneficial both for religious institutes looking to attract new members, and also for former volunteers looking to preserve the spiritual depth and sense of community they had experienced during their volunteer service. As the authors of the *Horizon* article put it:

> Experience has shown that women's religious congregations thrive when women join their volunteer programs. Volunteer programs give sisters new, energetic platforms for sharing their charisms and have resulted in powerful collaborations between a congregation's active ministry and efforts to promote new vocations. (Mulembe and Lackie 2016)

More widespread and publicized ways of linking religious institutes whose members want to hand on their charism to a new generation with Catholic former volunteers who are searching for a way to "figure out where I'm moving forward to" would meet the deepest desires of both the former volunteers and the vowed religious in the orders.

6

Other Factors Influencing Religious Vocations

Thu T. Do

ABOUT ONE IN ten never-married Catholics say they have considered priesthood or religious life (Gray and Gautier 2012). What really influences young Catholics to decide to enter religious life or the priesthood? Considering a vocation and committing to it is a lifetime process. Research indicates that the path Catholics take in developing an interest in a religious vocation, then discerning and seeking out that vocation is complex and that there is no one typical environment that helps to produce religious vocations. Discernment usually occurs in different environments that influence candidates in different ways.

The stereotypical candidates are likely to be members of a family that attends Mass regularly and to be active in their parishes beyond the worship services, as discussed in Chapter 3. They are more likely to participate in various activities of parish youth ministry and to attend Catholic schools. Moving on to college, these candidates are more likely to participate in the various religious and ministry activities offered by campus ministry, as was explored in Chapter 4. In all of these environments, they have the opportunity for discussion and encouragement of religious vocation, prayer and devotional practices, witnessing religious vocations, and learning about ministry through voluntary ministry and services.

Indeed, it takes a village to lead young Catholics to discern and decide to live a religious vocation. This chapter summarizes the research on these and several additional aspects that may influence women and men religious in their religious vocational decision during their childhood and young adulthood: attending Catholic primary and secondary schools, being active in parish life, and participating in campus ministry and volunteer activities during college. The chapter presents findings from various studies conducted by CARA on religious vocations and their influences. Where possible, it also makes comparisons to a national survey of never-married U.S. adult Catholics conducted by CARA in 2012.

FAMILY, PARISH, AND SCHOOL

It could be said that family, parish, and school are the three main institutions that influence vocational discernment among women and men. While all three institutions have an impact, either directly or indirectly, on the majority of religious during their religious vocational discernment, some religious may experience the influence of a particular institution more than others. Other religious relate that their vocational discernment occurred much later, at their workplace. Religious members related the impact of these environments on their discernment of a vocation (Gautier and Holland 2015):

As soon as I made my first communion, my grandparents encouraged me to become an altar server at my local parish. I remained an altar server until I became a junior in high school (which was a Catholic school). I also had an aunt who was a sister. We would visit her yearly when we would travel as a family to Quebec to visit extended family. I also really was inspired by several parish priests as I grew up.

Faith of my grandmothers; example of religious sisters who taught me in school, though I never had a personal friendship with one. . . . It was important to my parents to send us to Catholic school.

I attended Catholic schools from first grade through college. I'm certain that the influence of teachers as religious educators, connection to priests and to the parish, all of which my grade school facilitated, had a big impact on me. My parents are big advocates of Catholic schools. My older siblings all went to Catholic high schools and colleges. That was my environment growing up. My parents supported my own moral formation, loved me, and encouraged me to do service. These were promoted both at school and at home.

The Impact of Family on Religious Vocation

The family environment has an important impact on men and women religious' vocational discernment, as was explored in Chapter 3. That chapter concludes that the characteristics of families that nurture vocations to the priesthood or religious life are similar to those that nurture active lay Catholics who are happy and spiritually healthy adults. When asked what part of their family background had the most influence on their discernment of a religious vocation, men and women religious list the strong faith of their parents, regular Mass attendance, family love and support, prayer/devotion to Mary, and the strong faith of their grandparents, aunts, and uncles (Gautier and Holland 2015).

Discussions about a religious vocation are fairly common in some families but not in others. Half of the respondents to the Entrance Class of 2016 study revealed that starting a discussion with their family about religious vocation was easy for them, but the other half admitted that it was not easy. Obviously this subject is difficult for family members as well. Just three in ten respondents said that their mother and other family members had ever spoken to them about a vocation and even fewer, one in five, said that their father had ever spoken to them about a vocation (Gautier and Ngundo 2017). In general, men religious were more likely than women religious to find it easy to discuss their religious vocational discernment with their family members.

The Impact of Parishes on Religious Vocation

Catholic parishes provide many activities that can impact one who is discerning a vocation to religious life or priesthood, including religious/spiritual practices, religious education, youth group movements, and the presence of vowed religious and priests. CARA has been conducting in-pew surveys in more than one thousand U.S. Catholic parishes over the last twenty years, with the participation of more than 375,000 parishioners. When evaluating different aspects of worship in their parishes, most responding parishioners (88 percent) agree that their parishes provide good or excellent liturgies and sacraments (Wittberg 2012:160). More than two-thirds of responding parishioners report that their parishes offer at least *some* priority to providing opportunities for devotions such as rosaries, Eucharistic adoration, and small group prayer experiences. More than four in five (82 percent) agree that fostering priestly or religious vocations should be at least "somewhat" of a priority for the parish.

Although there is no way to measure how much effort parishes make to promote religious vocations, the men and women religious often describe how much their connection and involvement in the parish life impacted their religious discernment:

My family was always involved in parish life, and my siblings and I all participated in at least two ways with parish life (altar serving and youth group). My parish community that I grew up in continues to be part of my family.

*My family was very active in the parish so we got to know the pastor and the Sisters
who lived nearby through this. This made me open to the possibility of having a religious vocation.*

*I never considered being a Sister in college. I had never met Sisters so it wasn't even
a thought. I loved doing youth ministry and was very active in my local parish's
youth group. Looking back, I now see how the seed of my vocation was planted
through my work at the parish, but at the time, I gave no consideration to the
thought of religious life.*

The Impact of Catholic Schools on Religious Vocations

Participation in Catholic schools is generally considered to have an influence on
the religious vocational discernment of young Catholics, which was described here
in some detail in Chapter 3. Indeed, CARA data show that those who attended
Catholic schools are more likely to be exposed to religious life during school, to
participate in various faith-based activities, and to be in contact with religious
members or priests as faculty or campus ministers/staff (Cavendish, Cidade,
and Muldoon 2012; Gautier and Gray 2015). However, among the men and
women professing perpetual vows in religious life in 2016, while nearly half of
them attended Catholic elementary and middle school, just more than one-third
attended Catholic high school and college (Figure 6.1). Even though the men and
women entering religious life and making final profession in 2016 are more likely

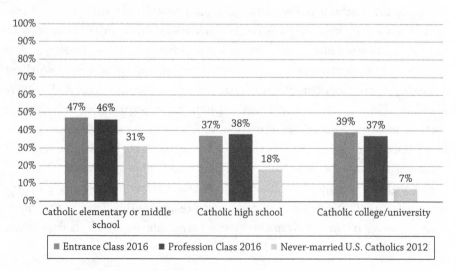

FIGURE 6.1. Attendance in Catholic Schools
Sources: Gautier and Ngundo (2017); Gautier and Do (2017); Gray and Gautier (2012).

than other U.S. Catholics to have attended Catholic educational institutions at some time during their education, most of them have little or no experience in Catholic schools.

Nevertheless, it is important to discuss how Catholic schools impact religious vocational discernment. Among men, having attended a Catholic secondary school is associated with a greater likelihood of having considered becoming a priest or religious brother. Among women, those who attended a Catholic primary school are three times more likely than those who did not to have considered becoming a religious sister (Gray and Gautier 2012). CARA finds that 76 percent of men and 57 percent of women who are currently religious or priests had considered becoming a priest or sister before attending college (Cavendish et al. 2012; Gautier and Gray 2015). Around two-thirds had considered a religious vocation at least somewhat seriously. This reality indicates that attending Catholic elementary and secondary schools often does have an impact on discerning a religious vocation.

While it may be difficult to disentangle and explain the reasons that lead to this difference, both men and women religious appreciated their experiences at Catholic school. Among the comments that religious shared when asked about what impacted their religious vocational discernment, Catholic school attendance appeared 132 times. For example:

Although not terribly religious, their cultural identification with Catholicism led my parents to send me to Catholic schools. My experience at a Catholic high school was instrumental in my vocation.

Being sent to Catholic schools made a huge difference in the development of my faith and the discernment of my vocation.

My mother made sure I attended Catholic parish grade school and all-girls Catholic high school. This gave me a foundation of faith life and exposure to consecrated women religious.

MASS ATTENDANCE AND RELIGIOUS DEVOTIONAL PRACTICES

Undeniably, Mass attendance and daily prayers are a major part of religious life. Most (90 percent) of the new candidates entering religious life report that daily prayers and religious practices are *very* important to them. Two-thirds report that Eucharistic adoration is *very* important to them, while four in five mention other devotional prayers, (e.g., the rosary) as at least *somewhat* important.

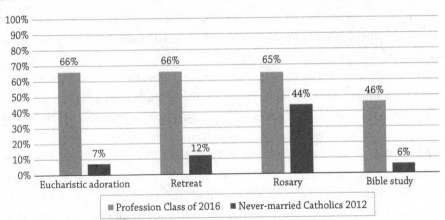

FIGURE 6.2. Participation in Religious Practices
Sources: Gautier and Do (2017); Gray and Gautier (2012).

The men and women religious who professed perpetual vows in 2016 were significantly more likely than other never-married Catholics to have participated in religious and devotional practices before entering religious life (Figure 6.2). Nearly nine in ten respondents participated in one or more of these prayer practices on a regular basis prior to entering religious life, while about one-third (32 percent) of never-married Catholics report participating regularly in one or more of these prayer practices.

The source of this interest may be due to several environmental factors: childhood experiences with their family, Catholic school attendance, or perhaps membership in parish youth groups. As Chapter 5 has already reported, the families of new priests, seminarians, and religious were three times more likely than an average adult Catholic in the United States to have attended Mass at least weekly when their children were growing up. Between 84 and 96 percent report attending Mass together as a family weekly or more often. The family members of the new priests and religious were more than twice as likely to say they pray together daily or more often and to say that religious faith was most important or among the most important things in their lives. Three in five family members say the family prayed the rosary together, either at home or elsewhere. Religious report these practices were influential to their religious vocational discernment:

Daily family prayer, especially the rosary, was most influential in my discernment. It was this daily family prayer which really helped me see the depth and richness of the Catholic faith, lived with fidelity and union with God through all of the joys and sorrows of daily life. *The witness of the faith of my parents and older siblings was very influential.*

Devotion to Our Lady family Rosary daily mass with my father, my mom's encouragement and prayers for my vocation family as important.

I think that we grew up, praying together every day—with the rosary, and went frequently to Mass. Our Catholic faith was really important to our family and the little traditions meant a lot to us kids when grown up. Also, I knew that they would support me with my decision to enter religious life.

In addition to Mass attendance and religious practices within the family, the families of religious members were often engaged in their faith in more public ways. Eight in ten were active in parish life. Two in three of the family members of religious report they participated in Eucharistic adoration at the parish. Given this environment, religious expressed how much this helped them develop their commitment to Mass attendance and religious devotions:

As a family we lived an active sacramental life (weekly Mass and monthly confession) and prayer life (daily prayer) along with parish involvement.

My parents' fidelity to each other, their love for helping others, and their involvement in the parishes where we lived (we lived on military bases throughout my life). Out of these, probably their desire to serve others (both within and outside the parish) was the strongest motivation for me to desire to serve others as well. The faith aspect was not as strong, though; that came later.

Weekly attendance of Sunday Mass, i.e., belonging to a home parish, knowing personally the priests, sisters, and other parishioners. We felt at home at Church.

Men and women religious may have been required by their parents to attend Mass and practice their faith while they were living with their family, but those who went off to college and lived away from their parents no longer had this reinforcement for regular religious practice. However, CARA finds that weekly Mass and religious devotional practices were still important to religious members while they studied in college. No matter what housing and living arrangement they might have had, most of them continued to attend Mass at least weekly and regularly practice other devotions. While there is only a slight difference in the level of these religious practices between religious who had attended Catholic or non-Catholic high schools, religious attending Catholic colleges/universities are more likely than those attending non-Catholic institutions to attend Mass and engage in devotional practices (Table 6.1).

TABLE 6.1

Participation in Mass and Religious Practice, by Attendance at Catholic
Schools

	High School		College/University	
	Catholic	Non-Catholic	Catholic	Non-Catholic
	%	%	%	%
Mass	87	83	88	67
Eucharistic adoration	63	67	75	60
Rosary	61	69	68	65
Lectio Divina	33	31	42	26
Bible study	47	46	57	41
Retreats	69	65	75	61
Spiritual direction	57	60	81	45

Sources: Data from Cavendish et al. (2012); Gautier and Gray (2015).

Mass and devotional practices have an impact on religious vocational discernment. When asked "what was most influential in your vocational discernment?"
half of 883 women religious participating in the survey (Gautier and Gray 2015) reported that their prayer life and the sacraments were the most influential. Many
referenced Eucharistic adoration and daily mass together with many forms of private and public prayer:

*Adoration—I started stopping by the Church for a few minutes on my way home
from school. It was in the presence of the Blessed Sacrament that I heard the call,
and received the courage to respond.*

*The support of a prayer life that I received in college was important but more impor-
tant was the availability of Eucharistic Adoration (permanently on campus) and
the Mass (home parish was within walking distance during high school I attended
daily, this habit I continued in college as was possible).*

*The most influential thing was my prayer and reflection, the influence of spiritual
writers and the monastic tradition, and my desire to give myself in service to God
and all of creation.*

Likewise, men religious were asked "during college, what kept you motivated in
pursuing a vocation to priesthood and/or religious life?" Religious respondents
report that Mass and devotional practices motivated them in their religious vocation (Cavendish et al. 2012):

A regular life of prayer, especially the Mass, and regular conversations about the Lord and His plan. Spiritual Direction was also an immense help.

Attending daily Mass, daily holy hour, daily rosary, and confession, spiritual direction, and the Legion of Mary group.

Mass, praying in Jesus' Eucharistic Presence, prayer group, personal prayer, and Scripture.

My daily prayer of lauds, vespers, and the rosary complimented my daily attendance at Mass so that I remained dedicated to Our Lord.

DISCUSSION AND ENCOURAGEMENT OF RELIGIOUS VOCATIONS

The number of people that encourage young Catholics to consider a vocation is associated with their religious vocational consideration. Young Catholic men and women who have a number of people encouraging them to consider a vocation are twice as likely as those who have no one encouraging them to consider religious vocation (Gray and Gautier 2012).

Most men and women religious (87 percent) who recently made profession into religious life report that at least one person encouraged them to consider a vocation to religious life (See Table 6.2). Among the encouragers, half report that parish priests encouraged them to consider a religious vocation, followed by friends (45 percent), and religious sisters or brothers (40 percent).

TABLE 6.2

Women and Men Religious Encouraged to Consider Religious Life by Others

	Combined	Women	Men
	%	%	%
Parish priest	53	58	50
Friend	45	46	44
Religious sister or brother	40	48	34
Mother	27	23	31
Parishioner	24	24	24
Campus minister/School chaplain	21	19	23
Other relative	19	15	23
Teacher/Catechist	19	18	21
Father	18	15	20

Source: Data from Gautier and Do (2017:21).

The men and women who entered religious life in 2016 were also asked how much encouragement they received from various people when they first considered entering a religious institute (Gautier and Ngundo 2017). Respondents most frequently mentioned a spiritual director (95 percent), a member of their religious institute (94 percent), other men and women religious (94 percent), and/or a vocational director/team (92 percent) as at least "somewhat" encouraging them when they first considered entering a religious institute.

The influence of parish priests and parishioners on religious vocational discernment is echoed in various CARA studies. For example, when asked who encouraged them to discern their religious vocation during college, around two-thirds of religious respondents report that they received encouragement from parish pastors (Cavendish et al. 2012; Gautier and Gray 2015). Another two-thirds of newly professed candidates in religious life report being "somewhat" encouraged by their diocesan priests. Nine in ten also report having been "somewhat" encouraged by people in their parish (Gautier and Ngundo 2017). Recently ordained priests, seminarians, and men religious also report the encouragement from pastors and people in their parish (Cavendish et al. 2012):

> Experiences during high school and a good relationship with my pastor from my home parish, who continually checked up on me and spoke with me about discernment.

> My parish community was also very supportive of my discernment request.

> Sought out monthly spiritual direction from a parish priest. He continued to encourage me through social outreach, bringing Communion to the sick, and pastoral counseling.

> The priest at the Newman Center as well as the priest at my home parish.

While discussing a religious vocation among family members is not always easy, many religious say they did receive encouragement for considering a vocation to religious life from their parents or other family members. Around one-third of perpetually professed religious received at least "some" encouragement from their family. Men were slightly more likely than women to receive encouragement from family members in their discernment of religious life (see Table 6.2).

When asked how much encouragement they received from their family, half of the respondents of the Entrance Class of 2016 report that they received "very much" encouragement from their parents and around three in ten report that they received "very much" encouragement from other family members (Figure 6.3).

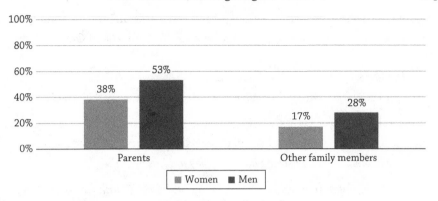

FIGURE 6.3. Encouragement to Consider a Vocation, by Gender
Source: Gautier and Ngundo (2017).

Men were more likely than women to receive encouragement from their parents and other family members.

In open-ended comments, men and women religious repeatedly mentioned the encouragement they received from family members as the most influential aspect of their family background (Gautier, Wiggins, and Holland 2015):

> *My dad sometimes asked if I had ever considered religious life but, at that time, I was always strongly opposed to becoming a religious. I think what was most influential in my family was just their faithful witness and encouragement. Also, my mother homeschooled all four children and taught us religion.*

> *The prayers of my grandmother and neighbors for priestly vocations, their encouragement to lead the rosary, my father's positive regard and comments about saintly priests in my country, my father's admiration towards the Jesuits, my grandmother's devotion and sincerely religious life, my mother's advice regarding careful discernment and openness to God's signs in my life.*

> *The support and encouragement I received from my parents and grandparents as I began my journey to become a brother. I would also say my parents' support by sending me to Catholic schools from grades 1-12 and to a Catholic college.*

In addition to parish pastors and family members, religious also mention receiving encouragement from friends, other men and women religious, and teachers and professors. Reported encouragement from friends is more likely to have occurred during their college years. One in seven religious responding to CARA's two surveys about the influence of college on vocation wrote that they were motivated to pursue a vocation because they had positive encouragement from their friends, other religious, or professors (Cavendish et al. 2012; Gautier and Gray 2015):

> At the most crucial point in my discernment, God blessed me with wise priests who gave me encouragement and pointed me in the right direction by their good counsel.

> I had a very strong group of Catholic friends to push and support me in all areas of my faith. This was also when I began to actually spend time just getting to know some religious sisters and seeing how real they are was helpful.

> The encouragement from my "spiritual family" at college (which was composed of friends, professors, priests, brothers, and sisters). Not only did they introduce me to the Lord and help with my re-version back to the faith (because I had become pretty lukewarm) but they taught me how to pray, taught me about the faith, loved me, and encouraged my discernment process. They were wonderful and gave me courage to discern.

> The liturgical life of the campus, the encouragement of my roommates and friends, and the Augustinians in administration and on the faculty.

WITNESSING RELIGIOUS VOCATIONS

Having the opportunity to get to know a priest or religious sister/brother on a personal basis is significant for men and women considering a religious vocation. Those who had such opportunities are twice as likely as those who did not to have considered a vocation (see Figure 6.4).

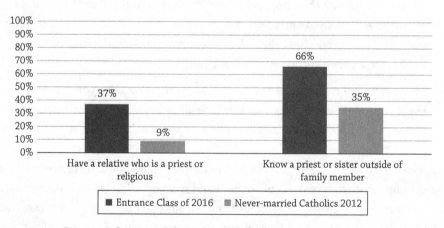

FIGURE 6.4. Priest or Religious as Role Model and Witness
Sources: Gautier and Ngundo (2017); Gray and Gautier (2012).

One common way of getting to know priests and religious is to be related to one. Men and women religious entering religious life are more likely than other never-married Catholics to have a priest/religious in the family. Many of the religious responding to CARA's surveys noted the influence of a relative who was a priest or religious as important to their religious vocation (Gautier, Wiggins, and Holland 2015):

My close relationship with my sister, who converted to the Catholic faith before I did and then entered the convent. I always saw her as an authority on religious things, so when I wanted to "get more serious" about my faith, I did so through her example. I ended up finding my vocation through volunteer work with her and her religious order. I ended up entering the same religious family.

My great uncle is a priest. From the time that I was 7 years to 12 years old he would come and stay with us for his two-week vacation. Although he never talked about what a priest is or what they do, it was by his living example that attracted me to him being "different."

Personal relationships with priests/religious: my aunt and godmother, who was a religious sister, and having several Jesuit family friends.

Parents also expose their children to religious life by inviting other priests or religious to their family for different family events:

My parents exposed us to religious life by inviting over the Franciscan or Passionist parish priests and taking us to Mass at the [Institute] Monastery. Also, my mother's insistence on letting the Holy Spirit guide you through life.

[My parents] also brought us to Mass often and invited priests over to our house frequently, where we could talk with them, learn the faith firsthand from them, and develop a good relationship that inspired trust and discernment. Since I did not know religious Sisters, diocesan priests were the ones who most shaped my discernment of religious life and my parents played a key role in helping this come about.

Several members of my extended family, particularly including my maternal grandparents, were friends with their parish priests as I was growing up. Being around priests at family get-togethers did a lot to humanize these priests and make them seem more relatable.

Besides getting to know priests or religious through their family, survey respondents also got to know them in the parishes where they were involved:

> My dad's discernment to the permanent diaconate and serving in our parish and being involved in our parish life (mom is secretary, dad is deacon) and knowing priests, sisters, and seminarians through our involvement.

> My family was very active in the parish so we got to know the pastor and the sisters who lived nearby through this. This made me open to the possibility of having a religious vocation.

> The relationship I had with our pastors/priests growing up and the OSF sister who was the director of religious education in our parish when I was a senior in high school.

Religious also note that attending Catholic schools sometimes gave them opportunities to see and get to know religious or priests on campus:

> I went to Catholic grade school and was influenced by the Franciscan sisters there. As an adult I had a blood sister who is a religious sister, as well as two cousins, also was close friends for many years with both a priest and a sister from the community I joined. I made the decision to become a religious after 25 years as an associate with my Community, though I had the thought on and off as a grade school student, however was discouraged by my mother. However I always knew that private prayer was important to both parents.

> My attendance at Catholic elementary and high school where I was in daily contact with the sisters during at least some of my primary and secondary education. Also, the support of my parents in pursuing my vocation and their own devotion to the faith even when it was economically hard for them.

> My parents sent me to Catholic school, so I was taught by Sisters. My first grade teacher, in particular, influenced my desire to become a Sister.

Witnessing priests or sisters on their college campus, whether in the classroom as professors or as campus ministers, had an influence on respondents' vocational discernment (Cavendish et al. 2012; Gautier and Gray 2015). But the likelihood that one knows a priest, sister, or brother while in college depends on the type of college one attends. Respondents attending a Catholic college or university were more likely than those who attended a non-Catholic college or university to have clergy or religious as professors or campus ministers (Table 6.3). More than eight in ten men and women religious who attended Catholic colleges knew priests or

TABLE 6.3

Had a Priest, Sister, or Brother as a Professor or Campus Minister, by College Type

	Catholic College		Non-Catholic College	
	Men	Women	Men	Women
	%	%	%	%
Professors	88	83	18	8
Campus ministers	90	84	59	45

Sources: Data from Cavendish et al. (2012); Gautier and Gray (2015).

religious through these roles, compared to far fewer among those who attended non-Catholic campuses.

Religious reported that the presence of priests, sisters, and brothers on campuses was an important factor in their decision to embrace a religious vocation later in life, as they witnessed these individuals faithfully living out their vocation. CARA's studies of the influence of college on men and women religious found that the respondents cited the "witness" of religious or priests ninety-six times. Specifically, two in five women respondents cited the personal witness of religious and priests as professors living out their vocations with happiness, integrity, and faithfulness as having a significant influence on their vocational discernment. This was cited by just over one-half (52 percent) of those who attended a Catholic college or university and nearly one-quarter of those who attended a public college or university. Respondents were also influenced by the personal witness of religious and priests as campus ministers. About one in five reported that the personal witness of their campus ministers as joyful and committed believers had an influence on their vocational choice (Gautier and Gray 2015).

A sister had an influence on me by her example and way of life. I went to her for spiritual direction and was very much in love with God and serving Him. Her dedication to poverty and the spread of God's mercy was also something I desired. Also, a priest helped guide me in the right direction as well.

I had four priests teach a theology class. The priestly witness was incredible. Seeing a priest a couple times a week and hearing them talk about the faith was a very affirming experience.

I had a Franciscan sister and a few Franciscan friars as professors. Their daily witness of joy, of faithfulness, and total commitment to the Lord was an encouragement and support to me in my discernment.

Simply their witness of religious life lived joyfully and faithfully. They guided me spiritually and sacramentally into a deeper relationship with Christ. The brothers witnessed to their life as religious in a profound way, especially through their joyful spirit and love of their students. The priest I had as a professor was inspiring in his commitment to service of God and neighbor.

YOUTH GROUP AND MINISTRY PARTICIPATION

Previous research has found that participation in a youth group is related to positive life outcomes (Smith and Faris 2002). Likewise, CARA research has found that religious-based parish youth programs have an influence on the vocational discernment of men and women religious. Many men and women entering religious life were active in their parishes before entering religious life. Most were more likely to participate in youth groups during high school than in primary school, but participation at both age levels influenced their vocational discernment.

CARA found that men participating in a parish youth group during the primary school years were 6 times more likely to consider becoming a priest or religious brother. In contrast, women participating in a parish youth group during the high school years were 9.6 times more likely to consider becoming a sister than those who did not (Gray and Gautier 2012).

It is apparent from Figure 6.5 that women and men religious are more likely than other never-married Catholics to participate in parish youth and young adult groups.

While respondents may have participated in part because of the encouragement of their parents and other family members, the activities in these programs had a

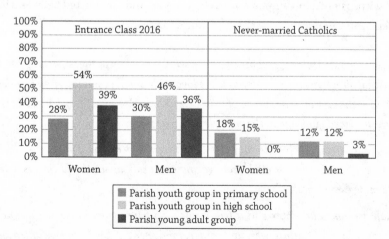

FIGURE 6.5. Participation in Parish Youth Group
Sources: Gautier and Ngundo (2017); Gray and Gautier (2012).

positive impact on their discernment of a religious vocation, independent of their family's influence (Gautier and Holland 2015):

> *After I was confirmed, I became a youth leader, and my brother's right hand man for helping to coordinate the youth group. It was assisting on retreats and helping plan youth meetings and going to youth rallies that gave me the idea that I could see myself doing this as a job and vocation.*

> *One of my brothers was active in youth group and went to the Steubenville Youth Conferences and always came back happy, so it made me want to do those things, too.*

> *While I have my parents to thank for being raised Catholic, most of my discernment happened with peers within a youth ministry context at a parish.*

Respondents reported that they continued their youth group involvement while in college, and these activities also had an impact on their religious vocational discernment (Cavendish et al. 2012; Gautier and Gray 2015):

> *During summers, I would return home and attend my local parish youth group as an older member. My group of Catholic friends who were practicing their faith grew, and I began to keep in contact with them during my final college years.*

> *The dream of ministering at a parish as a priest. Being involved in the life of parishioners. Working with the youth. Supporting the different parish social programs.*

> *The Sacraments and the vibrant youth in my parish. We would meet every night to pray rosary and get to know one another.*

CARA research also notes a positive association among male respondents between attendance at World Youth Day or a National Catholic Youth Conference and discernment of a priestly or religious vocation. Those who attended either of these events were more than four times likely than those who had not to say they had considered becoming a priest or brother. That study did not find a significant relationship among female respondents between attending World Youth Day or a National Catholic Youth Conference and discernment of religious vocation (Figure 6.6).

In the Entrance Class of 2016 study, however, which included both men and women entering religious institutes, respondents were also more likely than

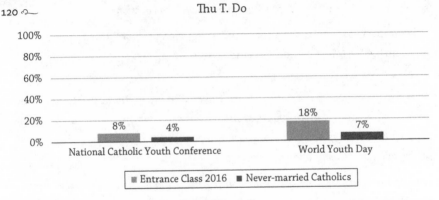

FIGURE 6.6. Participation in National/World Youth Events
Sources: Gautier and Ngundo (2017); Gray and Gautier (2012).

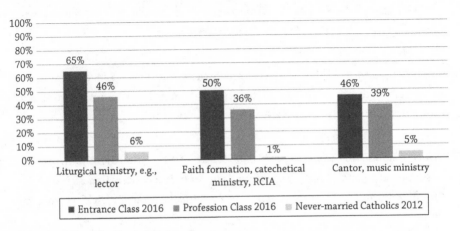

FIGURE 6.7. Participation in Ministry Programs
Sources: Gautier and Ngundo (2017); Gautier and Do (2017); Gray and Gautier (2012).

other never-married Catholics to have participated in the National Catholic Youth Conference and World Youth Day:

> I was also very much influenced by the example of Pope John Paul II, especially at World Youth Day in Toronto, in 2002.

> I really did not think of pursuing religious life while I was in college, however, I knew that I wanted to be involved in the church somehow. When I attended my first World Youth Day going into my senior year in college, I began to realize God was calling me to something more, but I did not know what that was.

Finally, professed religious respondents were much more likely to have participated in various religious activities than other never-married Catholics (Figure 6.7). Women who have participated in these ministry programs are more likely to consider becoming a religious sister than those who did not.

Eight in ten respondents of the Profession and Entrance Class of 2016 studies served in one or more ministries before entering religious life, either in a paid ministry position or as a volunteer, in comparison to only three in ten of other never-married Catholics. The most common ministry service reported was liturgical ministry (e.g., lector, extraordinary minister), followed by some form of faith formation. Both newly entering religious and those making perpetual profession are more likely than other never-married Catholics to have participated in these ministry activities. (Cavendish et al. 2012; Gautier and Gray 2015):

> *I think being involved with campus ministry and FOCUS and having friends tell me I would be a good priest. Leading a FOCUS Bible Study helped me realize how much I loved teaching faith and talking with people about their own faith journeys and sharing in their journey with them.*

> *I was involved in ministry during my entire college experience through confirmation retreats throughout my diocese. These opportunities allowed me to grow in my understanding of our faith and fall in love with it and the people of the church.*

> *Staying involved with the Church through service and ministry. Being a leader at the Catholic Center on Campus gave me responsibilities and helped me to see the Church in a different light. My friends were very supportive of me throughout my years of discernment.*

Two-thirds (67 percent) of the men and women in the Entrance Class and Profession Class studies participated in other volunteer work in a parish or in some other settings. Specifically, one in ten responding religious participated in religious institute volunteer programs (e.g., Mercy Corps or Jesuit Volunteer Corps). As Chapter 4 discusses, volunteer programs are associated with consideration of a religious vocation. Although fewer than one in twenty former volunteers (4 percent) have actually pursued a vocation to ordained ministry or religious life today, this is several times larger than the average among young Catholics who have not participated in volunteer programs. Additionally, two in five former volunteers (41 percent) have at least considered a religious vocation, which is much higher than the proportion among Catholic adults in general.

CONCLUSIONS

This chapter examined some of the other factors that influence the consideration of a vocation to religious life. Previous chapters have explored the ways that participation in parish life, attendance at Catholic schools, serving as a volunteer in a ministry experience as a young adult, and engagement in Catholic family life greatly impact religious vocational discernment. The discussion in this chapter pointed to research showing that activities such as regular Mass attendance and participation in religious devotional practices also have an influence on consideration of a vocation. Other factors, such as having the opportunity to discuss and receive encouragement from others to discern religious vocation, witnessing men and women religious, and being engaged in ministry and voluntary service as a youth and young adult also play a role in consideration of a vocation to religious life. While not every man and woman religious responding to the CARA surveys had the opportunity to experience all of these activities before they decided to enter religious life or the priesthood, all of these experiences reinforce one another and have an impact on Catholics' religious vocational discernment and decision-making.

The next set of chapters will look at some of the ways that religious life is evolving in the United States. Chapter 7 will present research about the lay women and men who associate with religious institutes to share in their ministry and spirituality without taking the vows to religious life. Chapter 8 will summarize CARA research on emerging religious institutes and lay ecclesial movements that have come into existence in the United States since the end of the Second Vatican Council. Finally, chapter 9 will explore international sisters and priests: religious women and men from other countries around the world who come to the United States to live, to study, and to minister to our increasingly diverse population.

7

Associates and Religious Institutes

Jonathon Holland, Mary Johnson, and Patricia Wittberg

WHO ARE ASSOCIATES? Most associates are laywomen and laymen who participate in some way in the spirituality and mission of a religious institute. While this may seem to be a relatively recent phenomenon, associates have existed since religious life began (Hereford 2012). During early Christianity, people would visit hermits who lived in the desert, bringing them food and supplies while seeking the spiritual knowledge that the hermits had acquired. After visiting the hermit, these early associates would go back to their homes and continue living as laypeople. Similarly, monastic communities have had lay associates called "oblates" for centuries, and the medieval Franciscans and Dominicans established "third orders" of lay members. Some of these third orders later became separate religious institutes.

As religious life has evolved and differentiated, so too has the relationship between religious institutes and those who associate with them. Some associates pray with the vowed religious, some work alongside them, while others donate financial resources to the institute. Historically, some ministries started by vowed religious were successful only because associates were willing to support them with time, expertise, and resources (Hereford 2012).

Each institute is free to define its own guidelines as to its associates' relationship with the institute. The institutes use many different terms to describe this relationship: associates, oblates, affiliates, companions, and third orders, among others. For the sake of brevity, the term "associates" will be used in this chapter, since more than half of the institutes refer to them by this term.

In recent times, there has been an increase in the number of people who wish to formally associate with religious institutes (Armstrong 2016; Ryan 2011). The North American Conference of Associates and Religious (NACAR) recognized that increase and commissioned the Center for Applied Research in the Apostolate (CARA) in the early 2000s and again in 2015 to study it.[1] This chapter uses the data from these studies to examine who associates are, their relationship with religious institutes, and the challenges that face them now and in the future.

METHODOLOGY

In 2000 and 2015, CARA contacted the leaders of religious institutes in the United States (and Canada, in the 2015 study) asking whether they had associates. Of the religious that responded to the 2000 survey, 53 percent had associates. Of the religious institutes that responded to the 2015 survey, 68 percent have associates, an increase of 15 percentage points. Of the institutes that did not have associates in 2015, 22 percent stated that they had had associates in the past, and 21 percent wanted to have associates in the future. Half of the institutes that said they have had associates in the past would like to have associates again in the future (and thus are included in the 21 percent).

After surveying the directors/coordinators of institutes' associates in 2015, CARA next sent each of them a second questionnaire to give to the associates and vowed religious in their institute. CARA received responses from 5,667 vowed members, 4,200 associates, and 207 third order/oblates, for a total of 10,074. Most of the responding religious institutes, 79 percent, are in the United States. Canadian religious institutes make up the other 21 percent of responses.

Two-thirds of these institutes began to have associates before 1990, while 13 percent did not include associates until after 2000. In the U.S. institutes with associates in the 2015 survey, 93 percent of the associates make a formal, renewable commitment, usually for one to two years at a time. Renewal rates for these commitments are quite high: 94 percent. Eighteen percent of the institutes offer associates the option of permanent commitment.

---

[1] The first survey was sent to directors of associates in 2000 and the second to associates and vowed religious in 2002. The second time the survey was done, all the surveys were sent in 2015.

Increasingly, associates are being led by an associate. In 2015, three in ten U.S. directors/coordinators of associates were themselves associates, an increase from the 11 percent reported in 2000.

Responding institutes in 2015 reported a total of 55,942 associates, more than double the number reported in the earlier study. Most institutes now have more associates than they have vowed members; the men's institutes have more than twice as many. Among the institutes that responded to the 2015 survey, 77 percent were women's institutes and 23 percent were men's institutes, but among respondents who returned the associates' survey, 90 percent were women and 10 percent men (Figure 7.1). Responding vowed religious are even more often female: Ninety-six percent were women while only 4 percent were men.

While the 2015 institute survey reports that associates were more ethnically diverse than they were in 2000 (73 percent Caucasian/white as compared to 84 percent in 2002), more than 90 percent of the respondents to the survey of associates and vowed religious in both years were Caucasian/white. The second largest group was Hispanic/Latino(a), which comprised 4 percent of the associate population and 2 percent of vowed religious population. African-Americans/blacks, Asians/Pacific Islanders, and Native Americans/American Indians comprised less than 2 percent of the population among both associates and vowed religious who returned the survey.

Vowed religious and associates are also highly educated. Two-thirds of associates had a college degree and 41 percent had gone on to graduate school.

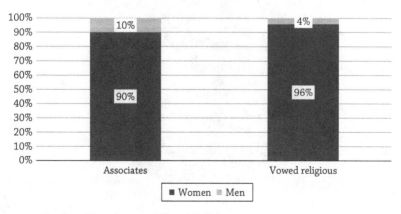

FIGURE 7.1. Gender of Associates and Vowed Religious
Source: Gautier and Holland (2016).

Over 90 percent of the vowed religious had a college degree and 82 percent had attended graduate school.

Both associates and vowed religious were older in 2015 than they were in the earlier study. The average age of associates in 2015 was 68, whereas in 2002 the average age was 61.

Associates connected to the men's institutes tend to be younger than those connected to women's institutes. Most of the recent growth in associates is in members who are between the ages of 60 and 80 (see Table 7.1). The number of associates under the age of 50 has not increased. Today, more than four-fifths (82 percent) of associates are over 60; only about 5 percent are under 50 (Figure 7.2).

Most (68 percent) of the 2015 respondents had become associates since 2000; only about one-third (32 percent) became associates before that year. The respondents were aware of—and worried by—the increasing age of both vowed religious and associates. When asked what they find most challenging about the

TABLE 7.1

Ages of Responding Associates

	Reported Associates	Under 40	40–49	50–59	60–69	70–79	Over 80
2002	25,500	1,020	3,315	6,630	7,650	5,355	1,785
2015	55,942	1,119	2,238	7,272	19,580	20,139	6,154

Source: Data from Gautier and Holland (2016).

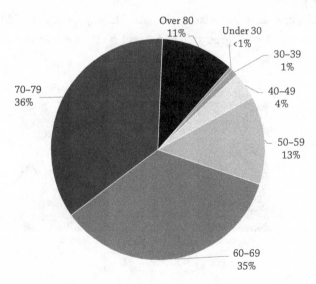

FIGURE 7.2. Age of Associates in 2015
Source: Gautier and Holland (2016).

future of the associate-religious relationship, the associates, vowed religious, and directors/coordinators of associates all are most likely to mention the age of the associates and vowed religious as their greatest concern. More than half spontaneously cited this in the responses to the open-ended question: "In your opinion, what are the most serious challenges your institute and the associate community face concerning the sustainability of the associate relationship?"

Inviting younger, more diverse ethnic backgrounds of men and women.

It seems that the associates are aging just as the vowed members are. Therefore, I don't know how the future of the associate membership will sustain itself.

Many associates are senior citizens and cannot attend all regular gatherings.

Older members find it difficult attending meetings. Attracting new members that are young and vibrant.

Associates and religious are not evenly distributed across their countries (Figure 7.3). Both tend to be consolidated in the Northeast, California, and Midwest of the United States, and in Ontario, Quebec, and Nova Scotia in Canada. In the years since 2002, however, associates are increasingly likely to be found in Florida, and less likely to be found in Michigan. Vowed religious are increasingly

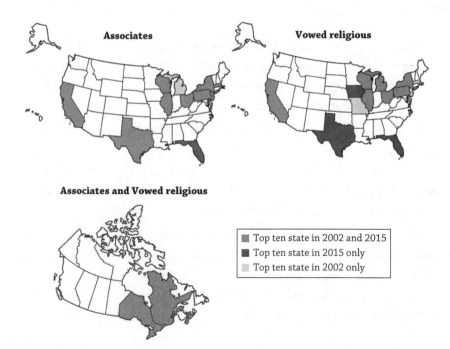

FIGURE 7.3. Location of Associates and Vowed Religious in the United States

likely to be found in Texas, Iowa, and Florida, and less likely than before to be in Massachusetts, New Jersey, and Missouri. This is similar to the rest of the Catholic population in the United States.[2]

One in ten associates and one in ten directors/coordinators list distance as the biggest challenge to their relationships with each other and their institutes.

> In our district, we no longer have religious living in our community. We must travel seven hours to meet with members of the order.

> The challenge from my point is the physical distance from the community. My contacts are limited to emails, letters, and phone calls. This presents a hardship for me as well as the whole community.

> The distance to the convent. . . . I wish I lived in the same city.

ATTRACTING ASSOCIATES TO THE INSTITUTE

Directors/coordinators of associates, associates, and vowed religious were presented with a list of items and asked how much each item attracts associates to the institute. As Figure 7.4 shows, a desire for a deeper spiritual life and the institutes' spirituality and mission are equally strong (over 90 percent) for all three groups:

> I am inspired and encouraged to enrich my personal, spiritual life and to strive to inspire others to deepen their baptismal commitment. I see the Associate movement as God's way of calling more of us to carry out the Gospel message in a special way.—Associate

> Although friendship has been the beginning of the relationship, which is personally rewarding, I find the depth of commitment by many to the mission of the community and a desire to that deeply in their own lives to be the most rewarding. The depth of spirituality and sharing of those aspects of their lives in prayer and conversation is a gift as well.—Vowed Religious

> Inspiring commitments/giftedness/stories of our members, strong unique worldwide ministries, spiritual connection, opportunities to grow in faith via various activities, various ways in which to participate and contribute, sense of belonging, life giving relationships, strong positive leadership, sharing the charism, spirituality of the congregation.—Associate

---

[2] According to data from the *The Official Catholic Directory* 1985–2015.

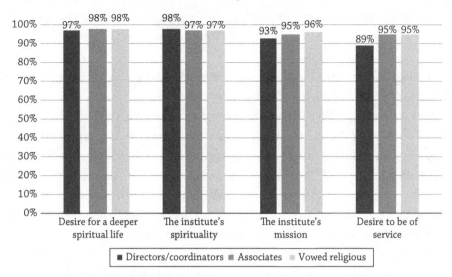

FIGURE 7.4. What Attracts Associates to the Institute? (Top 4 Responses by All Groups)
Source: Gautier and Holland (2016).

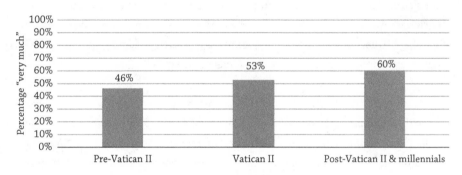

FIGURE 7.5. Desire for Community Attracts Associates, by Generation
Source: Gautier and Holland (2016).

The importance of these attractions varies, however, by several key demographic characteristics (see Figure 7.5). Younger associates were more likely than older ones to say that a desire for community "very much" attracts associates to the institute.[3] Associates in the United States were more likely than Canadian associates to say a desire for community attracts associates to the institute.

---

[3] Following previous research, CARA divides U.S. Catholics into "generations." The pre-Vatican II Generation, born prior to 1943, grew to adulthood before Vatican II. The Vatican II Generation, born between 1943 and 1960, passed their childhood in the pre-Vatican II Church, but experienced the post-Vatican II changes as teens or young adults. The post-Vatican II and Millennial Generations (born 1961– 1981 and 1982–1998 respectively) do not remember pre-Vatican II Catholicism. See Chapter 3 for a fuller explanation.

FOSTERING IDENTITY AND RELATIONSHIPS AMONG ASSOCIATES
AND VOWED RELIGIOUS

The directors/coordinators of associates were asked what they thought was most important for advancing the identity of the associates. Associates and vowed religious were asked what fostered the relationship between associates and vowed religious.[4] Two of the practices that almost all directors/coordinators agreed are important in fostering identity among associates is regular contact with vowed religious and with their fellow associates, and a formal orientation program (Table 7.2). The religious and the associate respondents agreed that these elements are important for fostering relationships, and they added two additional elements: participation in the institute's mission and participation in its prayer.

At the end of the survey, associates and vowed religious were asked what they found most rewarding about the associate-religious relationship. Four in ten associates and one-third of the religious mentioned the friendships they developed with each other as most rewarding. Similar proportions of associates and religious cited the advancement of the institute's charism. Other rewarding aspects mentioned by the associates included the opportunities for prayer and association with a faith-filled community; the religious also valued praying together as well as the new experiences, enthusiasm, and ideas the associates generate:

Involvement and interaction with the sisters and associates on a regular basis contributes significantly to the sustainability of the associates' community. The leaders composing the associate leadership team, shared prayer, community celebrations, various workshops, and sister/associate retreats create a oneness which aids in the sustainability of our associates.—Director/Coordinator

The love of the associates for the charism and mission is contagious. Their living of the charism questions us and calls us to be more fully alive in the spirit of our own Institute. Their relationship to the Founder and how they relate so deeply to his life puts us to shame. Their love for the poor (a dimension of our charism) is lived with real passion. The associates often bring us a new conversation and many of our men appreciate their presence at local community meetings, ongoing formation

---

[4] The question asked of directors/coordinators differed from the question asked of associates and vowed religious. Directors/coordinators were asked, "How important are these for advancing the identity of associate relationships?" Associates and vowed religious were asked, "How important do you think the following are for fostering relationships among associates and religious?" Although the questions' wording differed, the answers from which they could choose were the same, with one exception. Directors/coordinators could respond, "Volunteer service to the institute," while associates and vowed religious were not given that response option.

TABLE 7.2

How Important Are These for Fostering Relationships among Associates and Religious? (Percentage Responding "Somewhat" or "Very much")

	Directors/ Coordinators %	Associates %	Vowed Religious %
Regular contact with associates	93	94	93
A formal orientation program	93	93	95
Regular contact with vowed religious	92	93	95
Participation in institute's mission	89	95	95
Participation in institute's prayer	88	94	95

Source: Data from Gautier and Holland (2016).

and retreats. We offer them formation and mission possibilities, but it seems we receive much more than we give.—Vowed Religious

Most rewarding for me is the opportunity to interface and interact with members of the religious institute/community. I am grateful for their invitation to recognize and utilize our shared charism within the institute's community and in society.—Associate

The mindfulness of being a daily witness and representative of the spirituality and charism of the Institute. Living a life committed to faith in action connected to that spirituality and charism. Inclusion and participation in the annual Assembly with the vowed members is also a rich and rewarding experience in terms of maintaining relationships, friendships and sharing time together.—Vowed Religious

My relationship with this community has been a source of tremendous spiritual growth for me. I could not be who I am today without my shared history with my community. The times when we live most purely our call to love, freely, mutually, without concern for boundaries and roles, have been transformative, and, I believe, hold tremendous power to transform the world.—Associate

The identity of associates is thus closely tied to their relationship with the vowed religious of the institute. For many associates and religious, their mutual relationship is the most rewarding aspect of being an associate (Figure 7.6).

While younger associates and older associates largely agree on what is important to foster their relationship with the vowed religious, the younger associates were *more* likely than older associates to say that ongoing formation and participation in social activities are important for fostering it. The respondents also differed in how much associates and vowed religious participate in the activities that would bring them together. Older associates are more likely than younger ones to "very much" participate in prayer for associates and in commitment ceremonies. Older religious, similarly, are more likely to participate in associate commitment ceremonies and in mentoring associates. As these older, more participative associates and religious age, however, they will be less likely to maintain their former level of participation. The directors/coordinators in the 2015 survey noted that participation

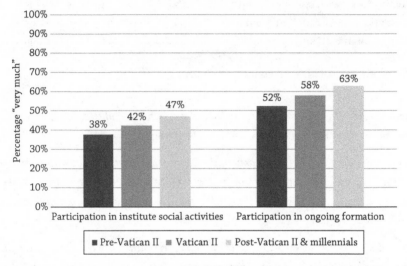

FIGURE 7.6. Important for Fostering Relationships among Associates and Religious, by Generation

Source: Gautier and Holland (2016).

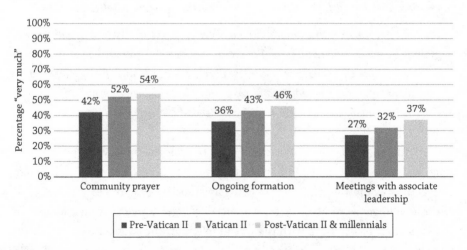

FIGURE 7.7. Associates Encouraged to Participate in . . . , by Generation

Source: Gautier and Holland (2016).

in associate meetings, in prayer/faith sharing with other associates, and in liturgies for associates has declined since 2000. The older associates and vowed religious were less likely to say that associates are encouraged to participate in community prayer, formation, and meetings with associate leadership (Figure 7.7).

ASSOCIATES AND LEADERSHIP

An important question for the future is whether and how the associates of a religious institute can or should assume more responsibility for the relationship. Nine in ten directors/coordinators believed that their institute's leadership model for associates is succeeding. Some 73 percent said they have a path for decision-making responsibilities with the associate community and 68 percent said that new models of leadership had emerged in the past five years. However, a third of the responding directors/coordinators and one in six of the associates themselves said that the most serious challenge their institute faced concerning the sustainability of associate relationship was a scarcity of associate leadership/commitment:

> *The most serious challenge that we are facing focuses on the level of commitment of the associates to be active participants in the transformation process. Another challenge that we face is the potential pool of future leaders for the associate leadership team.*—Director/Coordinator

Associate directors and coordinators were asked how well-prepared their associates were to assume responsibility for various areas of the associate-vowed religious partnership (Figure 7.8). They were the most likely to say their associates were at least "somewhat" prepared to take responsibility for gatherings and celebrations (89 percent), communication with associates (84 percent), and inviting others to associate relationship (84 percent). They were less likely to say that their associates were well prepared to assume responsibility for associate organizational leadership (69 percent), planning the future of the associate relationship (66 percent), and assuring its financial sustainability (42 percent).

Some of the associates' responses to the open-ended questions indicated an appreciation of the leadership opportunities they had been afforded or a desire to contribute more:

> *My self-confidence has blossomed and I have learned to participate as a co-director on team which is very rewarding.*—Associate

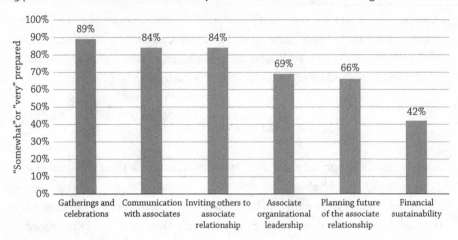

FIGURE 7.8. Preparedness of Associates to Assume Responsibility for . . .
Source: Gautier and Holland (2016).

Inability to participate fully in the process of envisioning the future by being in-
volved in key strategic, financial and governance committees (even as observers)
to be able to contribute experience and expertise to the evolution process. Many
of our associates are professionals and/or corporate managers and consultants
with many years of experience that could be more available to the sisters if
they would include us more often as resources in their planning and governance
*processes.—*Associate

But the older associates, especially, do not think they are encouraged by their institute to participate in planning and leadership opportunities (Figure 7.9).

Financial Sustainability

About 94 percent of associates and vowed religious agree that the associate community is sustainable for the next five years. However, some have concerns, especially
with regard to its future financial sustainability. In 73 percent of the responding
institutes, the institute covers most or all of the associate budget (Figure 7.10).
Associates are responsible for the entire budget in 15 percent of institutes.

How sustainable will this be in the future? One in seven directors/coordinators
of associates says that financial sustainability is the biggest challenge to the future sustainability of the associates. When asked if they think the associate community is financially sustainable for the next five years, 68 percent of directors/
coordinators of associates at least "somewhat" agree that their associate community is financially stable *with* institute support. However, less than half (43 percent)

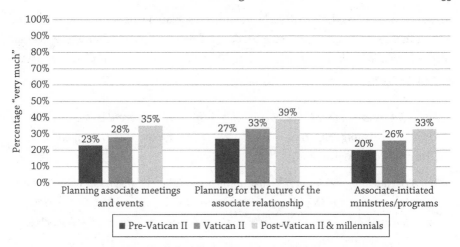

FIGURE 7.9. Associates Encouraged to Participate in . . . , by Generation
Source: Gautier and Holland (2016).

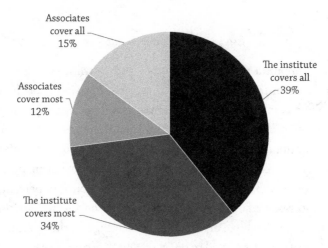

FIGURE 7.10. How Is the Associate Budget (Excluding Salary/Stipend and Benefits) Covered?
Source: Gautier and Holland (2016).

agree even "somewhat" that their associate community is financially sustainable *without* institute support. Directors/coordinators of associates in institutes of men and those in Canada are both more likely to say their associate community is financially sustainable. But for many institutes, as one director/coordinator put it, "Our community of associates is facing the very difficult task of establishing fiscal stability once the annual budget is no longer provided by the Sisters."

A tenth of directors/coordinators say that one of the lessons they have learned about the sustainability of the associates is that financial sustainability requires contributions from the associates. But when directors/coordinators were asked to measure whether the institute leadership, associate leadership, associates, and vowed members resist supporting associate financial sustainability, the average response was that each of these groups is neutral—neither completely resistant nor supportive.

> *Financial sustainability is key. We are currently being supported by the institute. This needs to change over time. We are working on ways to change this dynamic.*—Director/Coordinator

> *The Associate program is not self-sustaining financially. We are unable to make the donations yearly that would make that happen. I wish we could because without contributing more I feel we are a drain on the Congregation's finances.*—Associate

> *I think the most challenging is each remaining independent personally and financially, yet having a very special connection with ministry and mission and prayer.*—Vowed Religious

Associates and Institute Leadership

An important canonical question is whether and to what extent the associates should participate in the decision-making process, not simply of the associates, but of the religious institute itself. Currently, associates rarely participate in the institute's deliberations about financial or internal affairs: fewer than 10 percent of the directors/coordinators reported this kind of participation, and only 16 percent even "somewhat" agree that their associates want such participation. Similarly, few of the associates (21 percent) or the vowed religious (11 percent) reported that their institutes even "somewhat" encourage associates to participate in the institute's elected leadership. Participation in meetings on the institute's finances and internal affairs were reported to be "somewhat" encouraged by similarly small percentages (22 percent of associates; 15 percent of religious order members). Even participation in other leadership positions was said to be encouraged by only small percentages of respondents (24 percent of associate respondents; 18 percent of vowed religious respondents). Male religious institutes are somewhat more likely than the women's institutes to encourage associate participation in institute governance.

The Future of the Associate Relationship

About half of associates and vowed religious thought that the role of associates in associate leadership would increase in the next five years (Figure 7.11). There

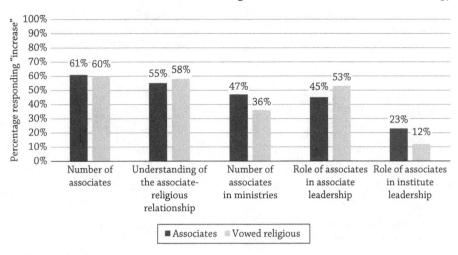

FIGURE 7.11. Aspects of Associate Life Likely to Increase in the Next Five Years
Source: Gautier and Holland (2016).

is a disjuncture, however, in the percentages of associates and vowed religious who think that the role of associates in institute leadership or ministries will increase.

Older vowed religious are more likely than younger vowed religious to say that the role of associates in associate leadership will increase. They are also more likely than younger vowed religious to say that the associate community is sustainable.

Sustainability of Associates

One of the greatest challenges facing the institute, according to directors/ coordinators, associates, and vowed religious, is attracting younger associates. Although half of the associate respondents to the survey agreed that the aging population of associates and attracting younger associates were the greatest challenges to their institute, just about half of associates (51 percent), and fewer than half of the vowed religious (44 percent), said they invite people to become associates either "somewhat" or "very much" (see Figure 7.12).

CONCLUSIONS

The findings from this research suggest that associate leadership, associates, and vowed religious continue to find strong value in the associate-religious relationship for their institutes and for individual associates and vowed religious.

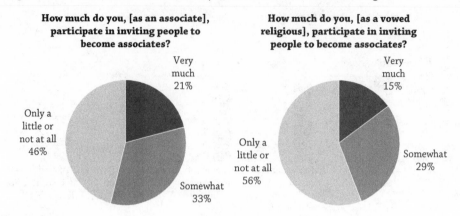

FIGURE 7.12. Inviting People to Become Associates
Source: Gautier and Holland (2016).

Associates and vowed religious grow deeply because of this relationship and be-lieve it will continue in the future:

> My firm belief is that association will continue to grow, as we carry the charism into the future with a firm direction in mind—the mission of our community. But less and less women are entering religious life in North America and those who we have are aging rapidly. That is so sad—tragic—and points us in the direction of making sure each associate knows her/his responsibility as an associate. Our covenants are to be taken very seriously, and to be renewed often as we move into different stages in our lives. Associates are aging, also, but new ones are joining us and adding new spirit to our ranks. Our "call" remains and will not fade away even if the number of sisters drops drastically.—Associate

> We could be on the threshold of looking at the associate program with fresh eyes and seeing the possibilities of a new way to be associated with the community. Our challenge is to take those initial steps of exploring the possibilities of how this new way could be practically lived out by those individuals and/or families called to serve Jesus Christ associated with our community.—Vowed Religious

> As the number of religious has decreased, the associates bring new life, energy, ideas, and enthusiasm to us, and are a sign of hope to me that our spirit and charism will continue through them in new ways. Their thirst for our spirituality make me appreciate more the richness that we have and deepen my love for it.—Vowed Religious

Moving forward, the keys to strong associate communities will be to:

- Continue a strong focus on the institute's mission and spirituality as a vital element for attracting associates and fostering relationships between associates and vowed religious of all generations.
- Be intentional in inviting younger and more diverse individuals to the associate relationship.
- Empower leadership from within the associate community to ensure sustainable leadership going forward.
- Plan for a sustainable future in the life of religious institutes and their associate communities.

8

New and Emerging Religious Communities

Patricia Wittberg

IN THE MORE than fifty years since the end of the Second Vatican Council, there have been numerous attempts to create new religious communities. Some of these attempts have developed into successful institutes, while others existed for only a few years before disbanding. Some have followed the long-established model of religious life: professing the traditional three vows, wearing a distinctive habit, living together in single-sex communities, and engaging in ministries of evangelization, teaching, retreat work, or monastic prayer. Others have experimented with new forms: mixed institutes of male and female or vowed celibate and lay members, charismatic covenant communities, and parish-based lay groups focused on spirituality or ministry. While the largest number of such communities have arisen in Italy and France (Rocca 2010; Landron 2004; van Lier 1998), many have sprung up in other countries as well—including in the United States.

In 1999, CARA compiled the first-ever directory of the new and emerging communities that had been founded in the United States since 1965. In 2006, a second edition was released, and in 2017 a third edition. All three were developed by contacting the territorial dioceses and Eastern-rite eparchies in the United States, and asking for the names and addresses of any new or emerging religious communities and lay movements headquartered within their boundaries. Criteria for inclusion in the directory were:

- Good standing in the diocese
- Having at least three or four members
- Founded since 1965 in the United States

141

CARA specifically asked the dioceses *not* to include any new groups that were formed and headquartered outside the United States, such as the Missionaries of Charity, Madonna Houses, or the Neocatechumenate, which may later have established a house or province in this country. The directory also did not include "daughter houses" of established Benedictine or Carmelite monasteries which, following their centuries-old practice, had sent some of their members into a diocese to begin a new monastery there.

The 1999 Directory contained 121 new communities that met these criteria; the 2006 Directory contained 142. Of the 121 communities in the 1999 directory, 24 (20 percent) had disbanded by 2006. Of the 142 communities in the 2006 directory, 29 (again, 20 percent) had disbanded or been suppressed by 2016. Three other communities (2 percent) that had been in the 2006 directory still exist but are no longer affiliated with the Catholic Church. An additional 12 communities (8 percent) also survive, but have dwindled to just one or two members and have no new probationary members in formation. In other words, of the 142 new religious communities and lay movements that existed in 2006, 44 (31 percent) had either ceased to exist, left the Church, or dwindled to just one or two members by 2016. On the other hand, 61 new communities were founded between 2006 and 2016, so that the 2017 directory contains the names, addresses, and descriptions of 159 emerging lay movements and communities of consecrated life.

COMMUNITY TYPE AND CANONICAL STATUS

The Catholic Church has established in Canon Law specific stages of recognition for establishing new religious communities or lay movements. The first of these stages is that of a Private Association of the Christian Faithful (Table 8.1). Private Associations are formed by the initiative of Catholic laypeople. They are under the authority of the bishop, who may speak positively about them, but they do not yet have official diocesan recognition. In the 2017 Directory, thirty-seven groups (23 percent) had Private Association status.

The next stage is obtaining official recognition by the local bishop as a Public Association of the Christian Faithful. In the 2017 Directory, fifty-nine groups (37 percent) had Public Association status. For some of these groups, being a Public Association is the final status they desire to attain, since it grants them the option of experimenting with new forms such as having both men and women members or both vowed and non-vowed members. For other groups, being a

TABLE 8.1

Current Canonical Status

	Percent	Number	Year Founded (Median Year)
Private association	23%	37	1997
Public association	37%	59	1994
Religious institute	18%	28	1980
Society of Apostolic Life	3%	4	1975
None or no answer	19%	31	1994

Source: Data from Wittberg and Gautier (2017).

Public Association is simply a transitional stage on the way to ultimately becoming a full-fledged Institute of Consecrated Life.

The third canonical stage of recognition is usually as an Institute of Consecrated Life, the type of religious institute most familiar to Catholics. Members profess public vows, observe the evangelical counsels of poverty, chastity, and obedience, and live in community. While twenty-eight groups (18 percent) in the 2017 directory had already achieved this status, another thirty-two (20 percent) ultimately wished to attain it. In addition to Institutes of Consecrated Life, the Church also recognizes Societies of Apostolic Life as an alternate stage of recognition. Members of Societies of Apostolic Life do not take religious vows but lead a life in common and commit themselves to a specific apostolate. Four (3 percent) of the groups in the 2017 directory were already Societies of Apostolic Life; another three (2 percent) wished to attain this status. Another form of canonical recognition is as a Secular Institute, but no group in the 2017 directory either had or desired to attain this latter status.

In general, the longer a new religious community or lay movement had been in existence, the more likely it was to have achieved the final status its members desired. Thus, the median years of founding for full-fledged Religious Institutes (1980) or Societies of Apostolic Life (1975) were earlier than the median year of founding for Public Associations (1994), or for Private Associations (1997).

MEMBERSHIP

Not all of the communities provided membership information. Of the 133 that did, over half (52 percent) admit only women, about one-fourth (22 percent) admit only men, and another fourth (26 percent) admit both men and women as members. Two-thirds (67 percent) have only vowed, celibate members, while one-third admit married and non-vowed single laypeople as full members. In about half of the groups, (53 percent) all the members make public vows—usually the traditional ones of poverty, chastity, and obedience, although 9 percent make the traditional Benedictine vows of obedience, stability, and conversion of life instead. In one-fourth of the groups (25 percent), all the members make private vows or promises, while in the remaining groups, members either make no vows or promises, or else different members make different kinds of commitment. In addition, a quarter of the groups also make a fourth vow or promise, usually of simplicity, Marian conse-cration, or service to the poor.

A Sampling of New Communities

Companions of Christ (St. Paul, MN)

Founded 1992

Public Association

Full Members: 22 diocesan priests

In Formation: 10 seminarians

All profess private vows, some live in community. Do not share funds in common.

Lifestyle and Apostolate: To build authentic fraternity among its priest members and to grow in holiness.

Disciples of the Lord Jesus Christ (Amarillo, TX)

Founded 1972

Religious Institute

Full Members: 34 women. *In Formation:* 8 women

All profess public vows, live in community, share funds in common, wear a habit.

Lifestyle and Apostolate: A contemplative charismatic community with an evangelistic apostolate giving retreats and parish youth missions.

Franciscan Missionaries of Jesus Crucified (Albany, NY)

Founded 1987

Public Association

Full Members: 2 men, 12 women

In Formation: 4 women

Other Relationships: 1 man, 4 women

All profess vows, some live in community. Do not share funds in common.

Lifestyle and Apostolate: To provide an opportunity for persons with disabilities to serve the Church in a community of consecrated life. To reach out to those who suffer and help them find meaning in their suffering.

Nazareth Farm (Wheeling, WV) Founded 1979

Full Members: 4 men, 4 women

Membership is for a limited term only

All profess vows of chastity, simplicity, prayer, and service, and live in community.

Do not share funds in common.

Lifestyle and Apostolate: Provides service retreats for teens and young adults in which they repair substandard housing. "We celebrate the richness of Appalachia and experience God through building relationships between our volunteers and the local community."

SPIRITUAL TRADITION

Over half of the communities reported following a specific spiritual tradition (Table 8.2). By far the most popular was Franciscan (23 percent), followed by Carmelite (7 percent), Benedictine (7 percent), Augustinian (4 percent), and Dominican (4 percent). Other spiritual traditions included Ignatian, Charismatic, Marian, Servite, Trinitarian, and Vincentian, but each of these was mentioned by

TABLE 8.2

Spiritual Tradition

	Percent	Number
Franciscan	23%	36
Carmelite	7%	11
Benedictine	7%	11
Augustinian	4%	7
Dominican	4%	6
Other traditions	14%	23
None or no answer	41%	65

Source: Data from Wittberg and Gautier (2017).

only a few communities. A large percentage (41 percent) either listed no particular spiritual tradition or did not respond to the question.

COMMUNITY LIFESTYLE

In the past, religious institutes have followed one of several different recognized lifestyles. Some institutes have been composed of hermits who live apart from each other in separate hermitages and spend the day in prayer and some sort of manual labor. Other institutes are monasteries, whose members live in community but observe the same daily schedule as the hermits: prayer and work. Still other institutes are evangelical, claiming a primary mission of preaching the Gospel and conducting retreats or parish missions. Finally, many institutes are apostolic, established to perform specific services such as teaching, nursing, or care for the poor.

In the 2017 directory, 7 percent of the groups claimed a focus—in whole or in part—on the eremitic (i.e. the hermit) lifestyle (Table 8.3). Another 13 percent claimed a monastic focus, in whole or in part; 23 percent claimed to be evangelical, and 63 percent claimed to be apostolic. Forty-three percent added a fifth focus, claiming to be "contemplative." Some communities chose more than one of these foci: Thirty percent claimed to apostolic-contemplative, 16 percent claimed to be apostolic-evangelical, 10 percent said they were contemplative-evangelical, and 8 percent said they were contemplative-monastic. Thirteen communities did not answer the question about which lifestyle their members followed, and 16 communities listed other foci.

TABLE 8.3

Community Lifestyle

	Percent*	Number
Apostolic	63%	100
Contemplative	43%	68
Eremitic	7%	11
Evangelical	23%	36
Monastic	13%	20
Other	10%	16
None or no answer	8%	13

* Percentages do not add up to 100 because communities could select more than one.

Source: Data from Wittberg and Gautier (2017).

There was considerable variation among communities—and sometimes even within a single community—in the degree to which the members share in a common life. In 78 percent of the communities in the 2017 directory, all or some of the members lived together; in 71 percent, all or some of the members shared funds in common. These percentages are approximately the same as they were in the 1999 and 2006 directories.

A number of common spiritual and ministerial themes emerged from an analysis of the charism, mission or purpose statements submitted by the communities, as well as from their websites. The most common themes or emphases were living in or fostering community, engaging in evangelization, devotion to Mary, working with youth, and Eucharistic Adoration. Of course, the fact that some communities did not mention a particular theme or emphasis in their mission statement or on their website does not mean that they do not value or promote this theme—they merely might not have mentioned it.

Comparison of the themes in the 2017 directory with those listed in the earlier directories reveals patterns of growing or lessening salience (Table 8.4). Of course the comparison cannot be exact: The 1999 directory, for example, did not examine websites, which many communities did not have at that point. Still, it is evident that some themes appear more frequently today than they did ten or fifteen years ago, while others occur less frequently. Mentions of evangelization,

TABLE 8.4

Common Thematic Elements in Community Statements and Websites*

	1999 %	2006 %	2016 %
Living in/fostering community	n.a.	n.a.	45
Evangelization/the New Evangelization	n.a.	22	43
Devotion to Mary	21	36	34
Working with youth	5	18	22
Eucharistic Adoration/Eucharist in general	20	25	33
Fidelity to the Pope or Magisterium	14	13	20
Holy Spirit/charismatic spirituality	13	18	16
Praying for priests and bishops	10	7	15
Community poverty/simple lifestyle	n.a.	31	13
Pro-life/anti-abortion	n.a.	9	13
Rosary/Divine Mercy Chaplet/other devotions	n.a.	17	8

* Percentages do not add up to 100 because many communities' mission statements and websites included more than one theme.

Source: Data from Wittberg and Gautier (2017).

working with youth, pro-life/anti-abortion work, and the Eucharist/Eucharistic Adoration consistently increased over the three time periods, while references to simple lifestyles and devotional prayers decreased. Marian devotion, fidelity to the Church/Magisterium, charismatic spirituality/the Holy Spirit, and praying for priests showed a mixed pattern, increasing at some times and decreasing or holding steady at others.

APOSTOLATES

Of the 140 communities in the 2017 directory whose mission statements or websites listed specific apostolates, relatively few mentioned engaging in one of the traditional ministries (teaching, nursing in hospitals, or social work) that religious institutes had performed in previous eras. The most commonly mentioned of the traditional apostolates was teaching in parish schools or private religious academies, but only 25 (16 percent) of the communities engaged in this apostolate (Table 8.5). Similarly, only 24 communities (15 percent) engaged in some form of health care ministry, primarily by caring for the sick or elderly in non-hospital settings or by serving as pastoral ministers in hospitals rather than as medical personnel there. Even fewer engaged in professional social work. Far more commonly, the communities listed conducting retreats, parish missions, or prayer groups, contemplation and prayer, or catechesis as their primary apostolates. Many

TABLE 8.5

Apostolate	Percent*	Number
Conducting retreats/missions/prayer groups	38%	61
Prayer/contemplation	29%	46
Catechesis/evangelization	23%	37
Work with the poor	22%	35
Parish work	21%	33
Teaching	16%	25
Health care (includes hospital chaplains)	15%	24
Social work	7%	11
"Active-contemplative"	25%	39
No answer	12%	19

* Percentages do not sum to 100 because many communities' mission statements and websites included more than one apostolate.

Source: Data from Wittberg and Gautier (2017).

communities made a point of stating that they followed an "active-contemplative" lifestyle, giving equal weight to contemplation or prayer and to their active ministry.

In comparison with the apostolates reported in 2006, a larger percentage of the 2016 communities reported engaging in retreat work (38 percent as compared to 23 percent), parish ministry (21 percent as compared to 11 percent), working with the poor (22 percent as compared to 16 percent), and ministry to the sick and elderly (15 percent as compared to 9 percent). For the other apostolates, approximately similar percentages reported engaging in them in 2016 as they had in 2006.

A Sampling of New Communities

Franciscans of the Eucharist of Chicago
Founded 2010
Public Association
Full Members: 1 man, 2 women
In Formation: 2 men, 8 women
All profess public vows, live in community, share funds in common, wear a habit.
Lifestyle and Apostolate: Daily Eucharistic Adoration, Mass, Liturgy of the hours; serve and live with the poor, evangelization through retreat work and teaching the poor Catholic schools and parishes.

Sisters of Life (New York, NY)
Founded 1991
Religious Institute
Full Members: 91 women
In Formation: 49 women
All profess public vows, live in community, share funds in common, wear a habit.
Lifestyle and Apostolate: a contemplative prayer life and apostolic works ministering to women vulnerable to abortion, retreats and educational seminars for married couples, healing ministry to those who have suffered abortion, pro-life education and evangelization.

Alleluia Community (Savannah, GA)
Founded 1973
Private Association
Full Members: 158 men, 172 women

In Formation: 20 men, 20 women

Other Relationships: 40 men, 45 women

All profess private vows, live in community, share funds in common.

Lifestyle and Apostolate: An ecumenical, charismatic community which operates its own K-12 school for the children of its members, runs a soup kitchen, and engages in prison ministry and pro-life work.

Hermits of Bethlehem (Paterson, NJ)

Founded 1982

Full Members: 2 men, 4 women

In Formation: 1 woman

All profess public vows, live in community, share funds in common, wear a habit.

Lifestyle and Apostolate: A Laura (colony) of Consecrated Hermits of Diocesan Right.

Each hermit lives in a separate dwelling on the same compound and dedicates his/her life to prayer and penance in the silence and solitude of the wilderness for the glory of God and the salvation of souls.

COMMUNITY ASPECTS ASSOCIATED WITH GROWTH
Community Size and New Members

The size of the new communities varies considerably. The median number of full members in each community was 9, with a range from one full member to 440 members. The median number of probationary members each community has in formation was 2, with a range of 0 to 113. As might be expected, groups of hermits are the most likely to be small in membership: Half had 6 or fewer members. Half of the monastic groups also had six or fewer members. Evangelical and apostolic communities, on the other hand, are more likely to be relatively large: Half of the evangelical communities had more than 15 members, while half of the apostolic communities had more than 12 members. Compared to previous directories, a somewhat larger percentage of 2016 groups reported having more than 15 members.

When it comes to attracting new entrants, the hermits and the monastic communities are the least likely to have no one at all in formation (Table 8.6). But they are also the least likely to have many new entrants, probably because they tend to be small in membership. Since half of the hermit and monastic groups have six or fewer full members, it would be highly improbable for them to have more members in formation than they have full members. In contrast, the apostolic and evangelical communities are more likely to have no one in formation, but they are also more likely to have over seven members in formation.

TABLE 8.6

Number and Percentage of Members in Formation, by Community Lifestyle

	Eremetic		Monastic		Evangelical		Apostolic	
	Percent	Number	Percent	Number	Percent	Number	Percent	Number
None	11%	1	14%	3	28%	9	30%	28
1-2	67%	6	43%	9	16%	5	21%	20
3-6	22%	2	33%	7	19%	6	21%	20
7 +	0%	0	10%	2	37%	12	28%	26

Source: Data from Wittberg and Gautier (2017).

Traditional Emphasis and New Members

What makes some religious communities and lay movements more attractive to new entrants than others? Many writers on religious life have speculated on this question. Insofar as the specific characteristics of a given religious community or lay movement are reflected in its mission statements and on its website, CARA's three directories may be able to provide an answer. A number of commentators have suggested, for example, that communities with a distinctive habit, or those that emphasize fidelity to the Pope and Magisterium, are more likely to attract new members than those without this emphasis. All three directories included information about whether the members of the emerging communities wore a habit and, if so, what the habit looked like. The mission statements and websites of the communities indicated whether their members emphasized fidelity to the Pope and the Magisterium. The directories compared the communities with these characteristics to the groups that did not wear a habit, or that did not emphasize fidelity to the Pope and Magisterium, to look for differences in the numbers they reported in formation.

Communities that wore habits and emphasized fidelity to the Pope or Magisterium were less likely to have no new members, and more likely to have many in formation (Table 8.7). The strength of the relationship between wearing a religious habit and having more new members was similar in the 2006 directory; the relationship between fidelity to the Pope or the Magisterium and having new entrants appears to have gotten even stronger since then.

Spirituality Emphasis and New Members

Other writers have asserted that communities with a strong emphasis on spirituality and prayer are more attractive to those considering religious life. To test this hypothesis, each edition of the directory compared the new and emerging communities

TABLE 8.7

Percentage of Members in Formation, by Selected Indicators*

	Religious Habit		Fidelity to the Pope and the Magisterium	
	No	Yes	No	Yes
	%	%	%	%
None in formation	43	18	33	6
1-2 in formation	16	26	20	31
3-6 in formation	8	24	18	22
7 or more in formation	16	26	19	34
No answer	18	5	10	6

* Percentages do not add up to 100 due to rounding.
Source: Data from Wittberg and Gautier (2017).

whose mission statements or websites emphasized Eucharistic Adoration or Marian devotion or identified the group as "contemplative" with communities whose mission statements or websites did not emphasize these things.

In the 2016 directory, communities whose mission statements or websites mentioned a contemplative focus, Eucharistic Adoration, or Marian devotion were less likely to have no new entrants, and more likely to have seven or more in formation (Table 8.8). Communities whose mission statements or websites mentioned that praying for priests and bishops was part of their charism or their ministry were approximately equally likely to have no one in formation as communities that did not express this emphasis, but they were still more likely to have seven or more members in formation. The relationships between new vocations on the one hand, and a contemplative focus, Eucharistic Adoration, or Marian devotion on the other hand replicated the relationships found in the 2006 directory. The relationship between Marian devotion and vocations was found in the 1999 directory as well.

Evangelization or Youth Ministry and New Members

Some writers have also hypothesized that communities working with young people would be more likely than those who do other types of ministry to attract new entrants. There were not enough communities in the 1999 directory with a special ministry to youth, so this hypothesis could not be tested for that year. In the 2006 directory, however, twenty-three communities reported working with youth. These twenty-three communities were no more likely than the rest of the communities to report having no one in formation, but they were significantly

TABLE 8.8

Percentage of Members in Formation, by Spirituality Indicators*

	Contemplative Focus		Eucharistic Adoration		Marian Devotion		Praying for Priests/Bishops	
	No	Yes	No	Yes	No	Yes	No	Yes
	%	%	%	%	%	%	%	%
None in formation	34	19	32	9	35	11	27	26
1-2 in formation	16	29	20	29	20	26	24	9
3-6 in formation	18	20	17	26	18	23	19	22
7+ in formation	18	28	20	29	18	30	20	35
No answer	14	4	10	6	10	9	10	9

* Percentages do not add up to 100 due to rounding.
Source: Data from Wittberg and Gautier (2017).

TABLE 8.9

Percentage of Members in Formation, by Apostolates*

	Work with Youth		Work with the Poor		Evangelization/ Catechesis	
	No	Yes	No	Yes	No	Yes
	%	%	%	%	%	%
None in formation	29	20	29	20	28	24
1-2 in formation	23	20	21	29	25	16
3-6 in formation	18	23	19	20	17	24
7 or more in formation	19	34	21	26	20	27
No answer	11	3	10	6	10	8

* Percentages do not add up to 100 due to rounding.
Source: Data from Wittberg and Gautier (2017).

more likely to report having more than seven new members. In the 2017 directory, there were thirty-five communities that listed working with youth as one of their apostolates (Table 8.9). As in the 2006 directory, the communities that work with youth were more likely to have seven or more new members in formation than those that did not work with youth. They were, moreover, less likely to have no one in formation. In all three editions of the directory, groups whose ministries involved working with the poor or engaging in evangelization and catechesis were somewhat less likely to have no one in formation and somewhat more likely to have seven or more new members.

GROWTH AND DECLINE

As was noted earlier in this chapter, twenty-nine of the emerging communities listed in the 2006 directory had dissolved by 2016. Another twelve had not grown beyond one or two members, and three were no longer affiliated with the Catholic Church. Of the surviving communities providing membership figures for both 2006 and 2016, thirty-three decreased in membership, eight remained the same size, and forty-three increased in membership, a few quite dramatically so. Nine communities more than doubled in size between 2006 and 2016, shown in italics in Table 8.10.

What are the characteristics of the nine communities with a greater than 100-percent growth rate? For most it was simply because they were small; five of the nine had had seven or fewer members in 2006. It is relatively easy to double a group's membership if it has only five or six members to begin with. The most rapidly growing community was a newly founded lay ecclesial movement with a charismatic spirituality. The second most rapidly growing group was a mixed community of four vowed religious sisters and forty-seven non-vowed men and women. The remaining two communities were religious institutes of women in the conventional sense of the term: the Dominican Sisters of Mary Mother of the Eucharist, and the Sisters of Life. Each grew from approximately fifty members in 2006 to over one hundred members in 2016.

Twenty communities grew by at least 50 percent between 2006 and 2016. The websites and mission statements of these communities displayed some differences

TABLE 8.10

Growth and Decline in Total Membership, 2006–2016*

Declining Communities		Growing Communities	
No change in size	8 communities		
−1% to −24%	14 communities	+1% to +24%	12 communities
−25% to −49%	10 communities	+25% to +49%	11 communities
−50% to −74%	7 communities	+50% to +74%	4 communities
−75% or more	2 communities	+75% to +99%	7 communities
Dissolved	29 communities	*+100% to +149%*	*4 communities*
Only 1 or 2 members	12 communities	*+150% to +199%*	*1 community*
No longer Catholic	3 communities	*+200% or more*	*4 communities*

* Figures include both full members and members in formation, 2006 and 2016.
Source: Data from Wittberg and Gautier (2017).

when compared to those of the communities that either had not grown at all or had grown by less than 50 percent. The faster-growing communities were more likely to describe themselves as living in or fostering community, engaging in the New Evangelization, working with youth, giving retreats or parish missions, wearing a religious habit, and being faithful to the Pope or the Magisterium. Among their spiritual foci or prayer practices, they were more likely to mention Eucharistic Adoration, Charismatic spirituality, praying for priests and bishops, and devotions such as the rosary or Divine Mercy chaplet. They were *less* likely to describe their community as contemplative or to say that they engaged primarily in an apostolate of prayer.

On the other hand, there was little or no difference between the rapidly growing groups and the rest in many of the ministries they reported: catechesis, teaching,

TABLE 8.11

Nineteenth-Century U.S. Religious Congregations of Women, Percentage Growth Within Ten Years of Founding*

Religious Initials and Location of Founding Community	Founded	Size of Community		Growth in First 10 Years %
		Initial	After 10 Years	
SC, Emmitsburg, MD	1809	8	94	+1,075
SL, Kentucky	1812	5	84	+1,580
SCN, Nazareth, KY	1822	24	74	+208
OLM, Charleston, SC	1830	3	14	+366
OSP, Baltimore, MD	1830	5	17	+240
BVM, Iowa	1833	5	19	+280
CSJ, Carondelet, MO	1836	4	25	+525
SP, Terre Haute, IN	1840	6	88	+1,366
SC, New York	1850	72	202	+180
CSC, Notre Dame, IN	1850	34	120	+252
CSA, Cleveland, OH	1851	4	22	+450
RSM, Hartford, CT	1851	4	10	+200
SC, Cincinnati, OH	1852	8	75	+838
OP, Racine, WI	1862	3	17	+467
SSJ, Watertown, NY	1880	4	8	+100

* Several communities (e.g., the Visitation sisters, the Carmelites, the Religious of the Sacred Heart of Jesus, and the Ursulines) are not included here because they routinely split into autonomous houses or monasteries when they passed a certain size. Male communities are also not included, as they were usually branches or provinces of European orders.

Source: Data from statistics compiled by Sister Catherine Ann Curry, PBVM, for Stewart (1994).

parish work, health care, pro-life activities, or work with the poor. Both groups were equally likely to report engaging in Marian devotions and having a simple lifestyle. There was also no difference between the rapidly growing and the other new communities in whether they claimed an Apostolic, a Monastic, an Evangelical, or an Eremitic lifestyle.

It is important to keep these growth figures in perspective. While nine of the groups in this directory more than doubled in size since 2006, and another eleven groups grew more than 50 percent during that interval, these growth rates are far less than occurred in the previous founding period of religious institutes in the nineteenth century. Table 8.11 gives the growth rates, where they can be determined, of some of the first religious institutes founded in the United States. None of the current groups come close to matching the rates of growth routinely experienced by the religious institutes that were emerging in the United States in the nineteenth century. And there are far fewer new and growing communities now than existed then.

CONCLUSIONS

The current population of emerging communities of consecrated life and lay ecclesial movements is a dynamic and changing one. The data for the most recent of the three directories were gathered in the spring and summer of 2016. Within the next decade, it is likely that some of the groups listed in that directory will disband and new communities will be created. Other groups will move, merge, or change the focus of their activities. A few, undoubtedly, will be the successful pioneers of the future of consecrated life.

As a whole, however, the growing communities profiled in the directories seem to reveal several trends and patterns:

- *The importance of a community lifestyle for religious communities.* Not only was this the most common theme in the mission statements and on the websites of the religious communities in the directories, but it was also one of the strongest differences between the new communities or lay movements that have grown more than 50 percent in membership between 2006 and 2016 and those that have not.
- *The importance of practicing, and teaching others to practice, contemplative prayer forms.* Contemplation as a common lifestyle continues to be chosen by over four in ten of the groups listed in both the 2006 and 2016 directories. Eucharistic Adoration is increasingly mentioned in the communities' mission statements and on their websites and was

one of the strongest predictors of which communities grew more than 50 percent between 2006 and 2016. Conducting retreats, parish missions, and prayer groups was also the most commonly mentioned apostolate for the new communities and was practiced by more communities in 2016 than in 2006. A full one-fourth of the communities stated that they were "active contemplatives," rather than simply listing an active apostolate.

- *The increased importance of evangelization and catechesis.* Mentions of evangelization as a thematic element in the new communities' mission statements and on their websites doubled between 2006 and 2016. In addition, catechesis was the third most commonly mentioned apostolate engaged in by the new communities and lay movements. Communities that focus on evangelization are more likely to have more than seven new members in formation, and are more likely to have grown more than 50 percent in membership since 2006.

- *The continued attraction of Franciscan, Benedictine, and Carmelite spiritualities.* In all three directories, these were the most frequently chosen spiritual traditions for new religious communities. Augustinian, Dominican, and Ignatian spiritualities, while important, were chosen less frequently.

- *The increasing importance of apostolates among youth and among the poor.* Ministering to youth and young adults grew consistently in importance between 1999 and 2016, and now ranks with ministry to the poor as chosen by over one-fifth of all the communities. This is significantly higher than the percentage of new communities involved in teaching, health care, or social work apostolates.

- *The attractiveness of particular models of religious life.* Communities whose members wear a religious habit and express fidelity to the Pope and the Magisterium, and those whose spirituality includes praying for priests and bishops, were more likely to have more than seven new members, and were more likely to have grown more than 50 percent in membership since 2006.

- *A less favorable environment for founding religious communities and lay movements.* While some of the new communities have experienced success and show promise of continuing to do so, this is a much smaller number and growth rate than occurred in the nineteenth century, when most of the older religious institutes in this country were founded. Most notably, the predominantly Catholic regions of the country that produced many new communities in the nineteenth century, such as New England and some of the Midwestern states, now no longer do so. This may be an indication of the secularization of parts of the country that formerly had a strong Catholic culture. Conversely, in other areas of the United States, the Church is experiencing growth. These areas may be the incubators of new religious communities in the future.

Previous historical studies found that consecrated life tends to go through repeated cycles of growth, decline, and rebirth (Cada et al. 1979). Each new wave of consecrated life is different from the preceding one (Wittberg 1994). Data in the three directories indicate that the Catholic Church in the United States may be on the threshold of another cycle of rebirth in consecrated life—new groups of Catholics committed to a shared spirituality and the evangelical counsels that will address the changing times, concerns, and needs of society, and the Church, in new and creative ways.

9

International Sisters and Priests in the United States

Mary Johnson and Mary L. Gautier

BY A WIDE margin, the United States has more total migrants than any other country in the world. In 2015, 46,630,000 people in the United States were born in other countries.[1] In mid-2016, the total U.S. population was 323.9 million people (Population Reference Bureau 2016). Thus, approximately 14.4 percent of the current U.S. population was born outside the United States.

Immigration to the United States is the backdrop of many of the Catholic Church's ministries of both public policy advocacy and direct service to the poor. While Catholic laity often staff these ministries, immigrant sisters and priests also accompany immigrants in a variety of ways today, as they have in the past. Historically, these sisters and priests came to serve their own ethnic group, but they often minister to others as well.

Who are these sisters and priests who have left their home country to serve in the United States? Where do they come from? How old are they? What are their ministries? To answer these questions, we turn to two recent studies: first, a Trinity Washington University/CARA study conducted in 2016 and 2017 that focused exclusively on international sisters, and the second a research project that CARA conducted between 2009 and 2012 for Oblate School of Theology on the topic of international priests.

---

[1] Conner, Phillip, and Gustavo López. "5 Facts about the U.S. Rank in Worldwide Migration," Pew Research Center FactTank. May 18, 2016, pewrsr.ch/2ifaedT.

What are the definitions of international sisters and priests according to the two studies? For the study on international sisters, the term is defined as a religious sister who was born outside the United States but who currently resides in this country. Some came to the United States as sisters, while others entered a religious institute after they arrived.

An international priest is defined in much the same terms in the CARA study for Oblate School of Theology. For that study, an international priest is a priest living in the United States who was born outside the United States. He may now be incardinated in a U.S. diocese or he may be serving as an extern priest in the United States (Gautier et al. 2014:13).

For context, it is important to note that sisters and priests coming to serve in the United States is not a new phenomenon. The new international sisters and priests in these recent studies follow earlier waves of sisters and priests from Ireland, Poland, Italy, Germany, French Canada, Mexico, and many other countries, who accompanied previous generations of immigrants or who entered the Church after immigrating themselves.

It is also important to note that the international religious women and men of today are part of the migration patterns that circle the world. In contrast to previous centuries when the most common pattern involved religious from Europe being sent to serve in the Americas, Asia, and Africa, today there is a larger influx of religious from the global South to the global North. The current phenomenon is more than just a simple reversal of mission, however. In fact, there is not just one story here—there are several and they are all compelling. Sisters and priests from the North and South cross paths, creating new patterns of international relationship and ministry, resulting in a dynamic and significant global network with the potential to bring even greater healing and hope to many parts of our Church and world.

A PERSONAL HISTORY OF INTERNATIONAL SISTERS

Before we look at trends and patterns, we need to remember that behind every statistic is a person with a history. And behind every social phenomenon are individuals who struggle and overcome obstacles as they face the circumstances of their lives and times. We begin here with two stories from co-author Sr. Mary Johnson's own family history. The stories will serve to illuminate the lives of two women who loved the country in which they were born, but who, upon immigration, entered into two new cultures, the culture of the United States and the culture of religious life. Like many immigrants, they helped build both the Catholic

Church of the United States and the nation itself, dying without ever returning home to see the family and friends they had left behind.

There were two waves of Irish immigration in my family—my parents, and some of their own aunts and uncles in the previous generation. My father had two aunts whom we would today call international sisters—one was his father's sister, the other was his mother's sister. Both immigrated to different U.S. cities and entered different congregations. Their congregational files, while sparse according to the custom of the day, contain details that give us some sense of the religious lives they lived and the contexts in which they ministered. They also put a human face on a social issue of historical and contemporary significance, and one that carries both pain and promise—the leaving of one's home country to build up religious life and the Catholic Church in one's new country in response to the call of the Gospel.

Sr. Margaret Clare Johnson S.S.J.

In a generation previous to my father's immigration from Ireland, four of his father's siblings had emigrated from Ireland to western Massachusetts. Among them was my father's aunt, Mary Catherine Johnson, who entered the Sisters of Saint Joseph of Springfield, Massachusetts, in 1917 at the age of twenty-four. Records indicate that she is one of the 137 sisters in the history of the congregation who were born in Ireland.

Mary Catherine Johnson became known as Sr. Margaret Clare Johnson S.S.J. Sister Margaret Clare received her habit on December 21, 1917, professed her first vows on December 20, 1919, and professed final vows on December 17, 1925. In her entrance statement, Sr. Margaret Clare listed English as the language she spoke and crocheting as a specialty of hers. Also, included in the file is the inventory of goods that were required for entrance. A dowry of $300.00 was expected. Sr. Margaret Clare brought $305.00 for the community fund.

She ministered as a "convent sister" in two assignments, Sacred Heart in Holyoke, Massachusetts, from 1920 to 1921, and St. Joseph in North Brookfield, Massachusetts, from 1922 to 1926. Her ministry as a convent sister involved home-making tasks of cooking, cleaning, answering the doorbell, and other extensive household tasks required for the upkeep of big convents with large communities of teaching sisters.

Unfortunately, Sr. Margaret Clare became ill in North Brookfield, Massachusetts, a rural community about thirty-five miles from Springfield, and died there from pulmonary tuberculosis at the age of thirty-three, after only nine years in religious life. The congregational file indicates that she may have been ill for only a month.

Because her illness seemed to have moved so rapidly, it appears that moving to the motherhouse or to a sanitarium was not an option. On May 13, 1926 she was anointed. On May 17 she was described as "very low," and the next day, Sr. Mary of the Holy Family was sent to the convent to care for her. On June 17, at 9:00 p.m., Sr. Margaret Clare experienced a "peaceful and happy death" in North Brookfield, Massachusetts.

On the following day, Mother John Berchmans, the superior general, accompanied Mr. T.P. Sampson, the congregation's undertaker, to escort the body of Sr. Margaret Clare back to the Motherhouse of the Sisters of St. Joseph on Elliot Street in Springfield. That journey, one way, would have taken at least two hours or more, probably on unpaved roads as they travelled through the rural community of North Brookfield and the rural communities surrounding it. That evening, Sr. Margaret Clare lay in state in St. Thomas' Room at the Motherhouse until the funeral Mass was said the next morning, Saturday, June 19, at 8:00 a.m. The Mass was celebrated by Father J.W. Tobin, as Bishop Beaven, the bishop of Springfield, was in Chicago at the Eucharistic Congress at that time.

Sr. Margaret Clare is buried in the plot of the Sisters of St. Joseph in St. Michael's Cemetery in Springfield, Massachusetts. Many family members in Ireland survived her, including her own mother (my great-grandmother Margaret Shea Johnson) and her brother (my grandfather Michael Johnson). There is no photo available of Sr. Margaret Clare. While there was a group picture taken of the congregation in 1914, numbering 329 Sisters of Saint Joseph of Springfield, unfortunately no names were attached to the photo, making it impossible to determine which sister is Sr. Margaret Clare.

Sr. Mary Brendan O'Shea S.C.

Several siblings of my father's mother also immigrated to the United States from Ireland, in the generation previous to my father's immigration. They immigrated to Pittsburgh, and one of the siblings, Elizabeth O'Shea, entered the Sisters of Charity of Seton Hill, Greensburg, Pennsylvania, in 1912 at the age of twenty-three. Congregational records indicate that there were at least 103 Irish-born sisters in her congregation during the course of its history.

Elizabeth was the daughter of Thomas O'Shea and Catherine McMahon O'Shea. She was born in County Kerry in June 1888 and baptized in Ballyferriter Church on June 23, 1888. She entered on March 19, 1912 from St. John the Baptist parish in Pittsburgh, and received the habit and the name of Sr. Mary Brendan on June 21, 1912. She pronounced her vows on July 19, 1914.

Sr. Mary Brendan taught in many parochial schools in the Pittsburgh area and continued to teach until the June before her death. Her last teaching assignment was Resurrection School in Brookline, Pennsylvania. Sr. Mary Brendan died at the age of 70 on March 29, 1958 in the forty-seventh year of her religious life.

The annals of the motherhouse, Assumption Hall, for March 29, 1958 read as follows: "Sister Mary Brendan died this morning in Pittsburgh Hospital after an emergency operation. She had been recuperating at Assumption Hall and Seton Hill after a cataract operation. She seemed to be doing well, but about three weeks before her death she suffered what was diagnosed as an abdominal obstruction. Surgery was indicated; but the Lord saw fit to take her home." Another document in her file indicates that the cause of death was diverticulitis and peritonitis.

The Annals of Assumption Hall contain further details about her wake and funeral: "Many relatives and friends paid their respects to Sister during the time she was laid out in the parlor on the first floor and there were many present for her funeral. The circumstance of numbers is noteworthy when one realizes that Sister came to America from Ireland when she was quite young, leaving her family and friends behind. Yet it never fails to happen that these same little Irish Colleens are literally surrounded by 'cousins and more cousins' when any celebration is in order. And they can always be counted on at the time of death. God bless them for their many kindnesses."

Sr. Mary Brendan's funeral Mass was celebrated in Assumption Hall at Seton Hill and she is buried in the sisters' cemetery at Seton Hill. She left a sister and brother in Pittsburgh, a sister in Chicago, and two sisters and two brothers in Ireland. Her file contains a picture of her in 1920, as part of a group photo of the congregation at its 50th Jubilee celebration. She is pictured in the distinctive garb of the Sisters of Charity of Seton Hill.

These two women, the sister of my grandfather and the sister of my grandmother, came from the same parish, were born in the same village five years apart, and entered religious life within five years of each other. While they immigrated to different states and entered different congregations, and while their files describe different ministries and different lengths of life, they also point to customs, structures, institutions, and support and challenges of community and family. History hides from us now whether they were friends before they left Ireland, or if they corresponded or were allowed to correspond after they entered. We can surmise that Sr. Mary Brendan would have heard of Sr. Margaret Clare's untimely death from relatives in Ireland or Pittsburgh and would have grieved for the loss of such a young sister. What we do know from their histories is that their relationships with God, family, clergy, their institutes, and their ministries constituted the bonds of their lives.

We can now ask: What will future generations of scholars find in the files of the newest generations of international sisters and priests? What will mark their lives, giving them meaning and significance in responding to God's call and the needs of God's people in their time? Which bonds will provide the strength they will need to respond to new needs in new times? Those questions will be answered by future scholars, but for now their stories can help us to paint a portrait in broad strokes of the international sisters and priests in the United States today.

INTERNATIONAL SISTERS AND PRIESTS

We address these questions by using data from two different studies. The most recent is the first ever national study of international sisters in the United States. This study involved three pieces of research. The first was a survey of all religious institutes in the United States. The second was a survey of international sisters identified by the leaders of the religious institutes and the vicars for religious in all the dioceses of the United States. The third included twenty-six interviews and focus groups with international sisters conducted in the Northeast, the Midwest, the South, and the West.

Surveys were sent to 560 institutes of women (including monasteries), with a 60-percent response rate. The responding institutes included U.S-based institutes as well as U.S. units of international institutes, missionary orders, and apostolic and contemplative institutes. Institute leaders, vicars for religious, along with other individuals and organizations, identified over 4,000 international sisters. These sisters come from 83 countries across six continents. Well over 1,000 sisters responded to the survey (in English, Spanish, French, and Vietnamese), and at least 75 sisters from over 30 countries were interviewed either as individuals or in focus groups.

The other source of data for this chapter is a study is of international priests conducted by CARA for Oblate School of Theology. Like the study of international sisters, this study also employed multiple methods and data sets to describe the 6,617 international priests in the United States in 2012 (See Gautier et al. 2014). Findings from both of these studies, where they are comparable, are used here to describe international sisters and international priests.

Where Are They From?

Asia is the largest sending continent for international sisters, and Oceania the smallest. One in three responding international sisters (33 percent) was born in one of the Asian nations (Figure 9.1). Among the Asian international sisters, Vietnam accounts for 44 percent of the international sisters; the Philippines, 24 percent; and India, 23 percent.

Among European sending nations, Ireland accounts for 41 percent, Poland 18 percent, and Italy 10 percent. From Africa, 38 percent of the sisters are from Nigeria, 16 percent from Uganda, over 10 percent from Kenya, and 10 percent

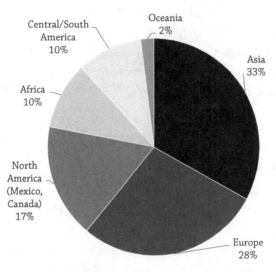

FIGURE 9.1. International Sisters' Place of Origin
Source: Johnson, Gautier, Wittberg, and Do (2017).

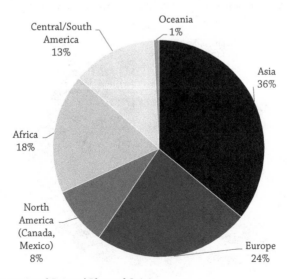

FIGURE 9.2. International Priests' Place of Origin
Source: Data from USCCB Secretariat of Child & Youth Protection (2012).

from Tanzania. From Central/South America, the four largest sending countries are Brazil, Colombia, El Salvador, and Peru. Thirteen percent of the sisters come from Mexico. And from Oceania, 71 percent of the sisters come from Australia, and 14 percent from Samoa.

Like international sisters, international priests come from many nations (Figure 9.2). The largest group comes from Asia, followed by Europe, Latin America/Mexico, and Africa. Very few come from Canada or Oceania. As of 2012, the majority of the 6,617 international priests reported by U.S. dioceses came from India, the Philippines, Nigeria, Ireland, and Mexico. Historically, Ireland had been the largest sending nation of international priests, but the largest group of international priests now comes from India. Poland, Vietnam, Colombia, and Spain are also major sending nations.

How Old Are They?

International sisters are typically much younger than U.S.-born sisters, whose average age nationally is in the high seventies. The average age of responding international sisters was fifty-eight, with half of them being fifty-five years of age or younger (Figure 9.3).

International priests, like international sisters, are younger than their counterparts. The average age of an international priest is fifty-three, while the average age of all priests is sixty-three. On average, international priests have been ordained for twenty-five years at the time they come to the United States, which means that they come with a good deal of experience in priestly life and ministry.

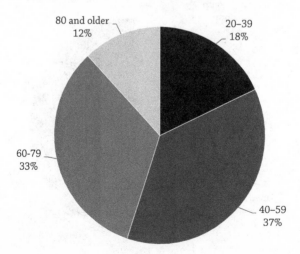

FIGURE 9.3. Age Distribution of International Sisters
Source: Johnson, Gautier, Wittberg, and Do (2017).

How Old Were They When They Came to the United States?

International sisters in the survey were age thirty, on average, when they came to the United States. Half of responding international sisters were age twenty-nine or younger when they arrived in the United States (Table 9.1).

In contrast to international sisters, international priests tend to be a little older when they arrive in the United States, averaging thirty-four years of age at the time of their arrival.

What Year Did They Come to the United States?

More than half of the international sisters (54 percent) reported entering the United States in 1992 or later (Figure 9.4). A quarter (25 percent) reported entering this country from 1966 to 1991, and one in five (21 percent) reported entering the United States in 1965 or earlier. The respondents said they had been in the United States for an average of twenty-seven years, with 41 percent here for fifteen years or less and 20 percent here for five years or less.

Three in four international priests said they had come to the United States in the 1990s or later (Figure 9.5). In 2012, at the time of the survey, they had been in the United States for fifteen years on average.

What Was Their Pathway to the United States?

Almost 40 percent of responding international sisters entered their current institute outside the United States and then were sent to the United States for ministry

TABLE 9.1

Age at Arrival in the United States, International Sisters and International Priests

International Sisters*	%	International Priests**	%
Age 12 or younger	6	Under age 20	7
Age 13–25	32	Age 20–24	11
Age 26–35	32	Age 25–29	14
Age 36–45	17	Age 30–39	40
Age 46–55	9	Age 40 and older	29
Age 56 and older	4		
Average age at entrance to U.S.	30	Average age at entrance to U.S.	34
Median age at entrance to U.S.	29	Median age at entrance to U.S.	35
Range in age at entrance to U.S.	1–81	Range in age at entrance to U.S.	2–69

Sources: * Johnson, Gautier, Wittberg, and Do (2017); ** Gautier, Cidade, Perl, and Gray (2014).

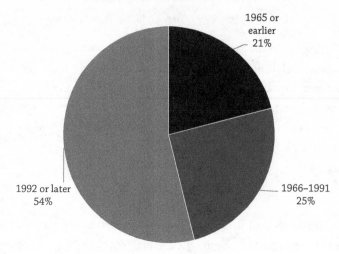

FIGURE 9.4. Year of Arrival for International Sisters
Source: Johnson, Gautier, Wittberg, and Do (2017).

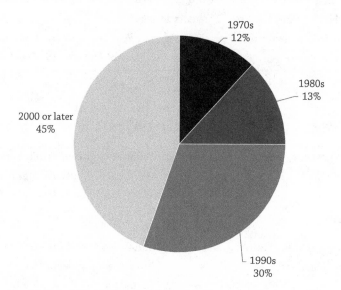

FIGURE 9.5. Year of Arrival for International Priests
Source: Gautier, Cidade, Perl, and Gray (2014).

(Table 9.2). Twenty-eight percent came to the United States before entering religious life. Thirteen percent entered their current institute outside the United States, then were sent to the United States for study. Ten percent were sent to the United States for religious formation.

A smaller number came to the United States via other ways. Six percent transferred to a U.S. province of their institute from another province outside the

TABLE 9.2

Pathways to the United States for International Sisters

	%
I entered religious life in this congregation outside the United States, then was sent to the United States for ministry	39
I came to the United States prior to entering religious life	28
I entered religious life in this congregation outside the United States, then was sent to the United States for study	13
I entered religious life in this congregation outside the United States, then was sent to the United States for part of my religious formation	10
I transferred to a U.S. province of my congregation from another province outside the United States	6
I transferred to my congregation in the United States from another congregation outside the United States	2
I came to the United States to enter religious life in the United States	2

Source: Johnson, Gautier, Wittberg, and Do (2017).

United States. Two percent transferred to their institute in the United States from another institute outside the United States. Finally, 2 percent came to the United States in order to enter religious life.

Latin American/Mexican respondents were more likely to belong to an institute outside the United States and to have been sent to the United States for ministry (see Figure 9.6). African/Afro-Caribbean respondents are more likely to belong to an institute outside the United States and to have been sent to the United States for study. Asian/Pacific Islander respondents are more likely to come to the United States before entering religious life.

Why Did They Come to the United States?

Thirty-five percent of responding international sisters reported that their superiors sent them to the United States for a particular ministry (Table 9.3). Fifteen percent reported that a priest/bishop from the United States requested sisters from their institute for ministry. Thirteen percent reported that their superior sent them to the United States to study. Nine percent came for religious formation.

Other reasons were reported by smaller percentages of respondents, some of whom came to the United States prior to entrance. Some came with their families, some at the invitation of family or friends, and some came to enter religious life in the United States.

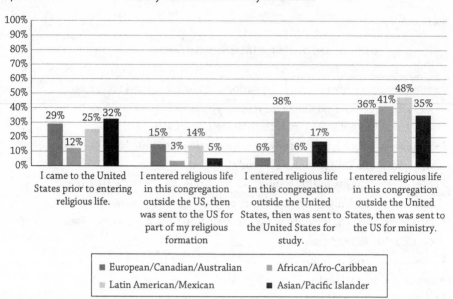

FIGURE 9.6. International Sisters' Pathways to Arrival, by Region
Source: Johnson, Gautier, Wittberg, and Do (2017).

TABLE 9.3

Reason/Purpose for International Sisters' Coming to the United States	%
My superior sent me here for a particular ministry	35
A priest/bishop from the United States requested sisters from my congregation for ministry	15
My superior sent me here to study	13
My superior sent me here for a part of my religious formation	9
I came to the United States with my family	9
A friend or family member invited me to come	8
I came to the United States to enter religious life	7
Other	5

Source: Johnson, Gautier, Wittberg, and Do (2017).

As can be seen in Table 9.4, international priests, like international sisters, also come to the United States for a variety of reasons. The majority (73 percent) said that the desire for ministry in this country "somewhat" or "very well" describes their reason for coming. About half (49 percent) responded to a request from an archbishop or bishop in the United States, with almost as many (44 percent) saying they responded to a request of their religious superior, and about one-third

TABLE 9.4

Reason/Purpose for International Priests' Coming to the United States*
(Percentage responding "Somewhat" or "Very well" for each item)

	%
Desire for ministry in the United States	73
Request of a U.S. arch/bishop	49
Request of my religious superior	44
Desire to pursue my educational goals	41
Request of my arch/bishop from home	32
Need to support my family/community	19

* Percentages do not sum to 100 because respondents were asked to evaluate how well
each item describes their reasons for undertaking ministry in the United States.
Source: Gautier, Cidade, Perl, and Gray (2014).

(32 percent) responded to an archbishop or bishop from their home country. The
desire to pursue educational goals was expressed by 41 percent, and the need to
support their family or community by 19 percent.

What Is Their Level of Education?

While international priests, obviously, hold advanced ministry degrees required
for ordination, the responding international sisters are also highly educated
(Figure 9.7). More than seven in ten international sisters earned an undergraduate
or graduate degree. More than one in ten (14 percent) completed some college.
Likewise, more than one in ten (13 percent) completed secondary school or less.

How Proficient Do They Consider Themselves to Be in the English Language?

Seventy percent of the responding international sisters are fluent or native
in English language skills. A quarter or more comprehend, speak, and write in
English at a minimum proficiency. Only 4 to 6 percent have no or limited English
proficiency. The longer international sisters stay in the United States, the more
fluently they master the English language.

Most international priests (60 percent) would have found help with U.S. language pronunciation helpful as they began their ministry in the United States;
45 percent said would find it helpful in their ministry at the time they were
surveyed. When asked about language study in a language other than English,
36 percent said it would have been helpful when they began ministry in this

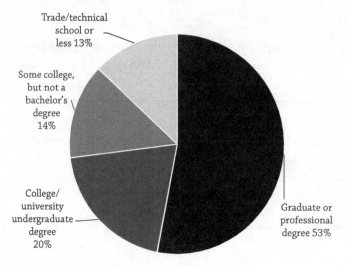

FIGURE 9.7. Level of Education for International Sisters
Source: Johnson, Gautier, Wittberg, and Do (2017).

country; 39 percent say it would have been helpful to their ministry at the time they were surveyed.

What Are Their Current Ministries?

Eighty-five percent of the responding international sisters were in active ministry. Of those, 21 percent served in parish/diocesan/ethnic group ministry (Table 9.5). Twenty percent served in hospital/health care ministry. Fifteen percent served in education, with 1 percent serving in campus ministry. Fourteen percent were students. Thirteen percent served their institutes in leadership, vocation, and formation work. Nine percent served in social service ministry, and 5 percent were contemplatives living in monasteries. Three percent responded as serving in other ministries, most of which are spiritual direction or retreats.

The data on current ministry for international priests is sparser. Most international priests (78 percent) ministered in parishes and nearly half of them were pastors: 34 percent pastored a single parish and 14 percent pastored more than one parish. A little more than a quarter (27 percent) were a parochial vicar or associate pastor. Just one in six was in a ministry outside a parish, such as chaplaincy in a hospital, school, or prison; serving in diocesan or religious institute leadership; or in education, campus ministry, social service, or spiritual direction. Just 4 percent were students and another 4 percent were retired from active ministry.

TABLE 9.5

Current Ministry of International Sisters in Active Ministry
(Percentage responding among those who are active in ministry)

	%
Parish/diocesan/ethnic group ministry	21
Hospital/health care ministry	20
Education	15
Student at U.S. colleges/school of theology	14
Congregational ministry/formation/vocational director	13
Social service ministry	9
Contemplatives	5
Other ministries	3
Campus ministry	1

Source: Johnson, Gautier, Wittberg, and Do (2017).

CONCLUSIONS

International sisters and priests bring many gifts to the Catholic Church in the United States. They come from many nations and numerous religious orders and dioceses. They respond to multiple needs through a wide variety of ministries. They are, on average, younger than those sisters and priests born in the United States, while bringing high levels of education and many years of experience in ministry.

How these sisters and priests are welcomed and sustained in Church life in the United States as they share their gifts makes a difference for themselves and for the Church. They follow in the footsteps of previous generations of international sisters and priests whose evangelizing mission built the Church in the United States and whose institutions helped build the nation.

They make contributions but also have needs for their mission, language training among them. Effective acculturation programs that prepare the sending and receiving groups are also essential as the diversity of the sisters and priests and the complexity of their lives and ministries become better known. Evaluation of these programs and the widespread sharing of those results are a particularly important strategy for the future growth of the Church in this country, including vocation ministry.

The Church and the nation are enriched today by the presence of international sisters and priests, who minister not only to their own ethnic peoples but to all of the people of God. They echo the witness of the unique lives of the two sisters presented in this chapter. While those sisters lived more than a century ago, their witness to living their religious consecration in a country other than their own speaks powerfully to our time.

Our sense of Church is and has always been enlarged by the good works and witness of those sisters and priests who minister in a nation not theirs by birth. Their presence within the wider immigrant population in the United States draws attention to the compelling issue of immigration reform. Their migration to this country calls to mind the complex and global migration of religious, across centuries and, today, across most of the world. The power of their witness is one that history must not forget, and one that the contemporary Church and society must not ignore.

10

Learnings for Vocation Directors

Thomas P. Gaunt

ↄ───

THE PREVIOUS CHAPTERS provide an in-depth examination of a decade or more of studies by CARA and others on the many influences on vocations to religious life and priesthood in the United States. This chapter summarizes many of the key findings from the research and offers some reflection questions that can be of value to religious communities, vocation directors, and others interested in promoting vocations to religious life. We can look at these influences in two ways: those that encourage and sustain the discernment of a vocation to consecrated life and/or priesthood in general, and those that invite and inspire women and men to pursue a vocation in a specific religious institute.

INFLUENCES ON CONSIDERATION OF A VOCATION IN GENERAL
Family Faith Life

Perhaps the most important influence in an individual's faith life is the religiosity of his or her family of origin. Having parents and extended family members who communicate their faith readily and practice their faith within their family through Mass attendance, prayer at meals, seasonal devotions (Advent, Lent, etc.) has an enduring effect on individuals. These family activities transmit faith and values in a way that few other relationships can. There are members of religious institutes that did not grow up in religious families, but they are few. Most men and women religious grew up in families where the practice of faith was clear, consistent, and encouraged.

For reflection:

- How does your religious institute foster family devotional practices (Advent, Lent, Feast Days, etc.)?
- Do the vocational materials of your institute address families, parents, siblings?
- Does your institute have ministries that engage families as well as individuals?

Parish Life

In addition, most religious grew up in a family that was active in their local parish, participating in parish devotions, ministries, and social outreach. The priests, sisters, and brothers who ministered in their parish were often guests in their homes. Many grew up knowing religious as friends of their parents and family. Their experience of parish was one of community and service; it was not only a place for Sunday Mass.

For reflection:

- If your institute is involved in parish ministry, how do the members of your institute engage the youth of the parish?
- Is there an active devotional life in the parish for teenage and young adult members?
- Are there service opportunities for teenage and young adult members?
- Are there reflection groups in the parish for young adults?
- Is there a conscious and deliberate effort to encourage individuals to consider consecrated life?

Catholic Schools

Catholic school education is also correlated with the discernment and decision to enter religious life, especially if the individual attended a Catholic high school and Catholic university. It is during adolescence and young adulthood that individuals usually consciously incorporate the faith of their family of origin as their own. Being in a Catholic educational institution at that time is key as a young person is exposed to and gets to know adults from outside his or her family who express their faith as educators, campus ministers, coaches, etc. Faith is expressed and experienced far more readily and in every facet of a Catholic school's life than occurs in a public or non-sectarian high school or university.

For reflection:

- Do the high schools and universities sponsored by your religious institute have retreat programs for the students that appropriately incorporate the institute's spirituality and charism?
- Is the availability of spiritual direction offered and publicized at the schools?
- Are there service opportunities for the students, and are they linked to your religious institute's charism?
- Are there regular opportunities for the students to learn more about your religious institute's spirituality and life of prayer?
- Does your religious institute offer and widely promote a "Come and See" program for those expressing an interest in the institute?
- Is there a conscious and deliberate effort to encourage students to consider consecrated life?

Volunteer Service

Another potent factor for young adults who have discerned a vocation to religious life is the impact of a year or more of volunteer service after college. There are hundreds of volunteer service programs open to recent college graduates across the nation and many of these programs are sponsored by religious institutes. A common element in practically all of the Catholic-sponsored volunteer programs is some structured time for reflection and prayer every week on the experience of serving those in need. This regular reflection and prayer, often informally done with two or three other volunteers, encourages individuals to discern and grapple with a vocational call. Where is their faith leading them?

Alumni(ae) of faith-based volunteer service programs are far more likely to be actively engaged Catholics in later life: They are more regular Sunday Mass attenders, more likely to self-identify as Catholics, more likely to volunteer and donate to their parish and community organizations, and are less likely to experience divorce. An extraordinary number of former volunteers pursue a vocation as sisters, brothers, and priests. Some 10 percent of alumni and two percent of alumnae end up pursuing a vocation in religious life or priesthood, whereas only a fraction of 1 percent of their Catholic peers do so.

Each year four or five thousand young women and men join a faith-based volunteer service program for a year of service. They are probably the most identifiable pool of potential vocations to religious life in the United States. Sponsoring a volunteer service program (solely or jointly with others) should be an important consideration for every religious institute.

For reflection:

- Does your religious institute sponsor or co-sponsor a volunteer service program?
- If so, how does the program link the service with the charism of your institute?
- Is there a regular element of structured reflection and prayer in the program?
- Do members of your institute regularly interact and have a relationship with the volunteers?
- Does the program explicitly foster a discernment of a vocation of service in the Church (lay, religious, or cleric)?

INFLUENCES ON CONSIDERATION OF A PARTICULAR RELIGIOUS INSTITUTE

In discerning a vocation to religious life, there are hundreds of religious institutes, each with a particular history, charism, and ministry, that an individual might enter. What are the specific factors that draw an individual to one community or another? CARA research has identified several important factors: the witness and visibility of religious, a common life and prayer, the presence of younger members, and the inclusion of a variety of ethnic/cultural members.

Personal Witness and Visibility of Religious

In the CARA survey of those religious in formation, over half of those who attended a Catholic college or university specifically cited the personal witness of women and men religious living out their vocations with happiness, integrity, and faithfulness as having a significant influence on their vocational discernment. The witness of these religious faithfully living out their vocation as believers had a great impact on the vocational discernment of those who later entered religious life. In particular, individuals relate the personal witness of a woman or man religious to their specific religious institute.

A practical challenge is the *visibility* of women and men religious to those who may consider a vocation to religious life. How are they known and recognized? Religious habits or other distinctive garb is one way to be recognized, as are the use of the religious titles of sister, brother, or father. In small institutional or ministry settings religious may be readily known and recognized without a distinctive garb or title, but in large institutional or ministry environments how will people recognize the man or woman religious and their witness? And will their witness be associated with living a good Christian life, or will it be associated with the charism and ministry of their particular religious institute?

For reflection:

- How does someone recognize members of your institute? What is distinctive?
- Are there ways for your members to be more visible, more recognizable?
- Do members, at least some, regularly and consistently interact with young adults?
- Do those interactions project joy and engagement in their ministry, their community life?
- In what ways does your institute present itself on the internet and in social media?
- Is it easy for someone who is not familiar with your institute to locate it online and to navigate your site?

Community Life

Individuals who are discerning a vocation to religious life are seeking to *belong* to a community of faith: They desire to join a group of similarly inspired women or men. Living in community is a particular attraction especially in terms of sharing prayer, meals, and a common ministry with other members of the religious institute. CARA research has shown that these aspects of a religious institute are highly valued by the younger members of the institute. The challenge comes as older members of the institute may not place as high a value on these aspects, which may lead to a conflict with or a disappointment by the younger members.

For reflection:

- Is the community life of your institute inviting and attractive to young adults?
- How much does your institute emphasize community life?

- Does your community regularly invite young adults to participate in community prayer, meals, and activities?

Cross-Generational Commonalities

The age distribution of members within a religious institute may play a key role in the institute's ability to engage and attract new members. Many religious institutes have a median age of seventy-five years or older and may have gone a decade or more without a new member. For young adults discerning a vocation to religious life, it is quite the psychological and social challenge to join a community that is not one, but two generations older (a community of their grandparents' generation). Younger members are more likely to attract other young adults to the religious institute.

For reflection:

- Is your community willing to welcome and positively engage a younger member?
- Is your community willing to change and adapt itself to a multi-generational community?
- Does your institute's website show members engaging with young adults? Does it show members of different ages interacting?

Cross-Cultural Commonalities

As with the age distribution within a religious institute, the ethnic and cultural mix of the members is an important factor in attracting new members. Numerous religious institutes were formed in the United States during the past 150 years that drew their membership from specific ethnic or cultural groups. The ethnic and cultural mix of Catholics in the United States has dramatically changed in recent decades, presenting a challenge to communities that are ethnically homogeneous. The challenge for religious life is that the professed members of religious institutes on average are 90 percent non-Hispanic white, whereas almost half of those entering religious institutes are Hispanic, Asian/Pacific Islanders, African-American, or Native American. How does a religious institute change, adapt, or evolve in its ethnic/cultural identification and manner of life?

For reflection:

- Is your community willing to welcome and positively engage members of different ethnic and cultural backgrounds?
- Is your community willing to change and adapt itself to be a multi-cultural community?
- Does your institute's website show any ethnic diversity? Does it show members of different ethnicities/different cultures interacting?

In recent years there has been an increase in the number of women and men entering religious life who were not born in the United States. Some came to the United States when they were younger, along with their families, and others are coming to the United States specifically to enter a religious institute here. It is helpful to understand the increasing number of foreign-born religious in formation within the context of the larger native-born and foreign-born Catholic population of the United States. Over the past thirty-five years the proportion of adult Catholics who are foreign-born has gone from 10 percent to 27 percent of the population. So it should not be unusual for the newer members of a religious institute to be 25 or 30 percent foreign-born.

For reflection:

- Are your institute's members in formation reflective of the immigrant reality of the Catholic Church in the United States?
- What vocation efforts and communications of the institute are directed toward the immigrant Catholic population of the United States?
- Is there resistance in your institute to accepting new members who are foreign-born?

REFERENCES

Armstrong, Patti. 2016. "Lay Associate a Growing Trend." *OSV Newsweekly*, July 27, 2016. Accessed May 6, 2017. https://www.osv.com/OSVNewsweekly/Faith/Article/TabId/720/ArtMID/13628/ArticleID/20365/Lay-associates-a-growing-trend.aspx.

Behar, Ruth. 1990. "The Struggle for the Church: Popular Anticlericalism and Religiosity in Post-Franco Spain." In *Religious Orthodoxy and Popular Faith in European Society*, edited by Ellen Badone, 76–112. Rutgers, NJ: Princeton University Press.

Bendyna, RSM, Mary E., and Mary L. Gautier. 2009. *Recent Vocations to Religious Life: A Report for the National Religious Vocation Conference*. Washington, DC: Center for Applied Research in the Apostolate.

Berger, Peter. 1967. *The Sacred Canopy: Elements of a Sociological Theory of Religion*. New York: Penguin Books.

Brettell, Caroline B. 1990. "The Priest and His People: The Contractual Basis for Religious Practice in Rural Portugal." In *Religious Orthodoxy and Popular Faith in European Society*, edited by Ellen Badone, 55–75. Rutgers, NJ: Princeton University Press.

Cada, Lawrence, Raymond Fritz, Gertrude Foley, Thomas Giardino, and Carol Lichtenberg. 1979. *Shaping the Coming Age of Religious Life*. New York: Seabury Press.

Caudron, Fran, and Richard Rymarz. 2013. "Further Down the Road: Longitudinal Study of Retreat Leaders from Catholic Schools." *Review of Religious Research* 55, no. 3 (September): 529–530.

Cavendish, James, Melissa Cidade, and Ryan Muldoon. 2012. *The Influence of College Experiences on Vocational Discernment to Priesthood and Religious Life*. Washington, DC: Center for Applied Research in the Apostolate.

Conway, Jill Kerr. 2002. "Faith, Knowledge, and Gender." In *Catholic Women's Colleges in America*, edited by Tracy Schier and Cynthia Russett, 11–24. Baltimore: Johns Hopkins University Press.

Connor, Phillip, and Gustavo López. 2016. "5 facts about the U.S. rank in worldwide migration." *Pew Research Center FactTank*. May 18, 2016. Accessed June 20, 2017. pewrsr.ch/2ifaedT

Cook, Timothy J. 2001. "Recruitment, Preparation and Retention of Catholic High School Religion Teachers." *Journal of Catholic Education* 4, no. 4: 530–556. Retrieved from http://digitalcommons.lmu.edu/ce/vik4/iss4/1.

D'Antonio, William V., Michele Dillon, and Mary L. Gautier. 2013. *American Catholics in Transition*. Lanham, MD: Rowman & Littlefield.

del Fra, Lou, CSC. 2016. "How We Nurture Vocations among our Volunteer Teachers." *Horizon* no. 4 (Fall): 26–31.

Dolan, Jay P. 1985. *The American Catholic Experience: A History from Colonial Times to the Present*. New York: Doubleday.

Ebaugh, Helen Rose Fuchs. 1993. *Women in the Vanishing Cloister: Organizational Decline in Catholic Religious Orders in the United States*. New Brunswick, NJ: Rutgers University Press.

Ewens, Mary. 1989. "Women in the Convent." In *American Catholic Women: A Historical Exploration*, edited by Karen Kennelly, 17–47. New York: Macmillan.

Feldman, Kenneth A., and Theodore M. Newcomb. 1969. *The Impact of College on Students*. San Francisco: Jossey-Bass.

Fialka, John J. 2003. *Sisters: Catholic Nuns and the Making of America*. New York: St. Martin's Press.

Fitzgerald, Maureen. 2006. *Habits of Compassion: Irish Catholic Nuns and the Origins of New York's Welfare System*. Champaign: University of Illinois Press.

Fogarty, Gerald P. 2001. *Commonwealth Catholicism: A History of the Catholic Church in Virginia*. Notre Dame: University of Notre Dame Press.

Gallup Editors. 2013. "Most Americans Practice Charitable Giving, Volunteerism," December 13, 2013. Accessed August 18, 2017. http://www.gallup.com/poll/166250/americans-practice-charitable-giving-volunteerism.aspx?version=print.

Gautier, Mary L., and Melissa A. Cidade. 2010. *The Profession Class of 2010: A Survey of Women Religious Professing Perpetual Vows*. Washington, DC: Center for Applied Research in the Apostolate.

———. 2012. *Educational Debt and Vocations to Religious Life*. Washington, DC: Center for Applied Research in the Apostolate.

Gautier, Mary L., Melissa A. Cidade, Paul M. Perl, and Mark M. Gray. 2014. *Bridging the Gap: The Opportunities and Challenges of International Priests Ministering in the United States*. Huntington, IN: Our Sunday Visitor Press.

Gautier, Mary L., and Thu T. Do, LHC. 2016. *Women and Men Entering Religious Life: The Entrance Class of 2015*. Washington, DC: Center for Applied Research in the Apostolate.

———. 2017. *New Sisters and Brothers Professing Perpetual Vows in Religious Life: The Profession Class of 2016*. Washington, DC: Center for Applied Research in the Apostolate.

Gautier, Mary L., and Mark M. Gray. 2015. *The Influence of College Experiences on Women's Vocational Discernment to Religious Life*. Washington, DC: Center for Applied Research in the Apostolate.

Gautier, Mary L., and Jonathon C. Holland. 2016. *A Profile of the Associate-Religious Relationship in the United States and Canada*. Washington, DC: Center for Applied Research in the Apostolate.

Gautier, Mary L., and Bibiana Ngundo, LSOSF. 2017. *Women and Men Entering Religious Life: The Entrance Class of 2016*. Washington, DC: Center for Applied Research in the Apostolate.

Gautier, Mary L., and Carolyne Saunders. 2013. *New Sisters and Brothers Professing Perpetual Vows in Religious Life*. Washington, DC: Center for Applied Research in the Apostolate.

Gautier, Mary L., Jonathon L. Wiggins, and Jonathon C. Holland. 2014. *Incorporating Cultural Diversity in Religious Life: A Report for the National Religious Vocation Conference*. Washington, DC: Center for Applied Research in the Apostolate.

———. 2015. *The Role of the Family in Nurturing Vocations to Religious Life and Priesthood: A Report for the National Religious Vocation Conference*. Washington, DC: Center for Applied Research in the Apostolate.

Glazier, Michael, and Thomas Shelley, eds. 1997. *Encyclopedia of American Catholic History*. Collegeville, MN: Liturgical Press.

Gleason, Philip. 2001. "A Half-Century of Change in Catholic Higher Education." *U.S. Catholic Historian* 19, no. 1: 1–19.

Gray, Mark M., and Mary L. Gautier. 2012. *Consideration of Priesthood and Religious Life among Never-Married U.S. Catholics*. Washington, DC: Center for Applied Research in the Apostolate.

Gray, Mark M., and Paul M. Perl. 2008. *Sacraments Today: Belief and Practice among U.S. Catholics*. Washington, DC: Center for Applied Research in the Apostolate.

Hereford, CSJ, Amy. 2012. "Associates of Religious Institutes – A Way Forward . . . " *RCRI Bulletin* 7 (Spring): 4–20.

Hutchison, Patricia. 2001. *The Purposes of American Catholic Education: Changes and Challenges*. www.researchgate.net.

Information Please. 2016. Accessed August 4, 2016. http://www.infoplease.com/ipa/A0104673.html.

Johnson, Mary, Patricia Wittberg, and Mary Gautier. 2014. *New Generations of Catholic Sisters: The Challenge of Diversity*. New York, NY: Oxford University Press.

Johnson, Mary, Mary Gautier, Patricia Wittberg, and Thu Do. 2017. *Trinity Washington University/CARA Study: International Sisters in the United States*. Accessed March 17, 2017. http://www.ghrfoundation.org/news/report-international-sisters-in-the-united-states.

Kosmin, Barry A. and Ariela Keysar. 2006. *Religion in a Free Market: Religious and Non-Religious Americans, Who, What, Why, Where*. Ithaca, NY: Paramount Market Publishing.

Landron, Olivier. 2004. *Les communautes nouvelles: Nouveaux visages du catholicisme francais*. Paris: Editions du Cerf.

McNamara, Jo Ann Kay. 1996. *Sisters in Arms: Catholic Nuns through Two Millennia*. Cambridge, MA: Harvard University Press.

Medved, Mary, SNJM. 2005. "Ruined for Life: Transforming Lives, Discovering Vocations through Volunteer Programs." *Horizon* no. 4: 35–38.

Misner, Barbara. 1988. *Highly Respectable and Accomplished Ladies: Catholic Religious Women in America, 1790–1850*. New York: Garland.

Moore, Cecilia A. 2006. "'To Serve through Compelling Love': The Society of Christ Our King and the Civil Rights Movement in Danville, Virginia, 1963." *U.S. Catholic Historian* 24, no. 4: 83–103.

Moylan, Prudence. 1993. *Hearts Inflamed: The Wheaton Franciscan Sisters*. Privately printed, Wheaton Franciscans, 26 West Roosevelt, P.O. Box 667, Wheaton, IL 60189.

Mulembe, Katie, and Carol Lackie. 2016. "The Vocation Impact of Full-time Volunteering." *Horizon* no. 4 (Fall): 21–25.

Nygren, David, and Miriam Ukeritis. 1993. *The Future of Religious Orders in the United States: Transformation and Commitment*. Westport, CT: Praeger.

Oates, Mary J. 1985. "The Good Sisters: The Work and Position of Catholic Churchwomen in Boston, 1870–1940." In *Catholic Boston: Studies in Religion and Community*, edited by Robert E. Sullivan and James M. O'Toole, 171–199. Boston: Archdiocese of Boston.

———. 2002. "Sisterhoods and Catholic Higher Education, 1890–1960." In *Catholic Women's Colleges in America*, edited by Tracy Schier and Cynthia Russett, 161–194. Baltimore: Johns Hopkins University Press.

O'Connell, Marvin R. 1989. "John Ireland, the Vatican, and the French Connection." In *The Papacy and the Church in the United States*, edited by Bernard Cooke, 99–117. New York: Paulist Press.

Orsi, Robert. 1985. *Madonna of 115th Street: Faith and Community in Italian Harlem, 1880–1950*. New Haven, CT: Yale University Press.

Ospino, Hoffman. 2015. "Affirming a Vocation Culture in Hispanic Families." *Horizon* 40, no. 4: 13–15.

Pace, C. Robert. 1979. *Measuring Outcomes of College : Fifty Years of Findings and Recommendations for the Future*. San Francisco: Jossey-Bass.

Pascarella, Ernest T., and Patrick T. Terenzini. 2005. *How College Affects Students. A Third Decade of Research*, vol. 2. San Francisco: Jossey-Bass.

Pope St. John Paul II. 1990. "*Apostolic Constitution Ex Corde Ecclesiae: On Catholic Universities,*" August 15, 1990. http://w2.vatican.va/content/john-paul-ii/en/apost_constitutions/documents/hf_jp-ii_apc_15081990_ex-corde-ecclesiae.html.

Population Reference Bureau. 2016. *2016 World Population Data Sheet*. August, 2016. Accessed June 20, 2017. http://www.prb.org/pdf16/prb-wpds2016-web-2016.pdf

Rocca, Giancarlo. 2010. *Primo Censimento delle Nuove Comunita*. Rome: Urbaniana University Press.

Ryan, Zoe. 2011. "Associates Embrace Orders' Charism." *National Catholic Reporter*, September 27, 2011. Accessed May 6, 2017. https://www.ncronline.org/news/associates-embrace-orders-charisms.

Sabine, Maureen. 2013. *Veiled Desires: Intimate Portrayals of Nuns in Postwar Anglo-American Film*. New York: Fordham University Press.

Saunders, Carolyne, Eva S. Coll, and Thomas P. Gaunt, SJ. 2014. *Volunteer Introspective: A Survey of Former Volunteers of Two Vincentian Volunteer Programs*. Washington, DC: Center for Applied Research in the Apostolate.

Saunders, Carolyne, Thomas P. Gaunt, SJ, and Eva S. Coll. 2013. *Volunteer Introspective: A Survey of Former Volunteers of the Catholic Volunteer Network*. Washington, DC: Center for Applied Research in the Apostolate.

Segale, Sister Blandina, SC. 1948. *At the End of the Santa Fe Trail*. Milwaukee: Bruce.

Smith, Christian, and Robert Faris. 2002. "Religion and American Adolescent Delinquency, Risk Behaviors and Constructive Social Activities." *A Research Report of the National Study of Youth and Religion*, no. 1. Accessed June 24, 2017. http://youthandreligion.nd.edu/assets/102504/religion_and_american_adolescent_delinquency_risk_behaviors_and_constructive_social_activities.pdf.

Stewart, George C., 1994. *Marvels of Charity: History of American Sisters and Nuns*. Huntington, IN: Our Sunday Visitor.

The Official Catholic Directory. 1985–2015. Berkeley Heights, NJ: P.J. Kenedy & Sons.

Thompson, Margaret Susan. 1989. "Sisterhood and Power: Class, Culture and Ethnicity in the American Convent." *Colby Library Quarterly* 23, no. 3 (Fall): 149–175.

Trent, James W., and Leland L. Medsker. 1968. *Beyond High School; A Psychosociological Study of 10,000 High School Graduates*. San Francisco: Jossey-Bass.

U.S. Conference of Catholic Bishops. 2012. Respondent Characteristics, Service Volunteering." Part I of *Survey of Youth and Young Adults on Vocations*. http://www.usccb.org/beliefs-and-teachings/vocations/survey-of-youth-and-young-adults-on-vocations-part-1.cfm.

U. S. Conference of Catholic Bishops Secretariat of Child and Youth Protection. 2012. *International Priests Database*. Washington, DC: USCCB.

Van Lier, Rick. 1998. *Les nouvelles communautes religieuses dans L'eglise catholique du Quebec*. Montreal: Universite Laval.

Wittberg, Patricia. 1994. *The Rise and Fall of Catholic Religious Orders: A Social Movement Perspective*. Albany: State University of New York Press.

———. 2006. *From Piety to Professionalism—And Back? Transformations of Organized Religious Virtuosity*. Lanham MD: Rowman and Littlefield.

———. 2012. *Building Strong Church Communities: A Sociological Overview*. Mahwah, NJ: Paulist Press.

Wittberg, Patricia, and Mary L. Gautier. 2017. *Emerging U.S. Communities of Consecrated Life since Vatican II*. Washington, DC: Center for Applied Research in the Apostolate.

Yanikoski, Richard A. 2010. "Catholic Higher Education: The Untold Story." *Origins* 39, no. 36: 588–594.

INDEX